D1649002

SHE ENGINEERS

Outsmart Bias,

Unlock your Potential,

and Create the Engineering Career

of your Dreams

STEPHANIE SLOCUM

Paperback Edition
Copyright © 2018 Stephanie Slocum

ISBN: 978-1-7320701-0-3

All rights reserved. No part of this publication may be reproduced, distributed, or transmitted in any form or by any means, including photocopying, recording, or other electronic or mechanical methods, without the prior written permission of the publisher, except in the case of brief quotations embodied in reviews and certain other non-commercial uses permitted by copyright law.

Although the author has made every effort to ensure that the information in this book is correct and accurate at the time of publication, the author and publisher do not assume and hereby disclaim any liability to any party for any loss, damage, or disruption caused by errors or omissions, whether such errors or omissions result from accident, negligence, or any other cause.

This book is written with the intent to share information based on research and personal experience of the author. While all stories based on the author's personal experiences are true, names and other specific details have been modified to protect the privacy of the individuals involved.

The reader assumes all liability resulting from use of advice or techniques provided in this book. The author and publisher assume no responsibility for your actions or the results accrued from the advice in this book. Mention of specific reference material, parties, or organizations herein does not imply their endorsement of this book.

www.SheEngineersBook.com
stephanie@engineersrising.com

Edited by: Sharon Honeycutt
Book design and interior formatting by Jen Henderson:
www.wildwordsformatting.com/
Cover design by Ida Sveningsson: www.idafiasveningsson.se/

DOWNLOAD THE
AUDIOBOOK FREE!

READ THIS FIRST

Just to say thank you for purchasing my book,
I would like to give you my audiobook 100% free!

Go to www.sheengineersbook.com/audiobook

DEDICATION

This book is dedicated to the following people:

My daughters

Claire, Madeline, and Eliza: May you grow up to honor who you are, and choose your own path in life. May you always have the courage to try new things, fail, and try again.

My husband

I could not have written this book without your generous support. Thank you for not thinking me crazy when I declared I was going to write a book to help other women in engineering in my "free time".

My parents

You taught me anything is possible if I set my mind to it and instilled in me the confidence to reach for my dreams. I am grateful for everything you have and continue to teach me.

My grandpa

You are the original engineer in the family who really was a rocket scientist. I wish you had been able to see the finished book. May you rest in peace.

This book is in honor of women everywhere who have the courage to chart their own course

TABLE OF CONTENTS

INTRODUCTION

Attending an awards event for architectural and engineering design projects in 2016, I literally bumped into a man as I worked my way towards the drink station in the packed venue and found myself in work-related conversation with him. After a few minutes of small talk and discussion of the projects which were up for awards, we exchanged business cards. He looked at mine and said:

"I wouldn't have thought you are an engineer."

Flash back ten years prior, to when I had completed the structural engineering design for a small addition at a local elementary school. As part of structural engineering design services, we periodically visit our construction sites to observe the work. This was my first-ever site visit as a solo representative of my employer on a project I had designed.

Clad in a hardhat, steel toed boots, and wearing safety glasses, I arrived at the job trailer to introduce myself to the contractor with whom I had corresponded but not yet met. As we walked out to the site, he said "You must be an engineer because your dad or brother own the firm. We don't see many women engineers here."

Flabbergasted by his statement —I didn't have any immediate family in-state, let alone in the same firm—and not knowing what else to do, I laughed it off and quickly corrected the assumption that I had those type of work connections.

I am a female engineer. I love what I do. I love the impact I have on countless lives in my chosen field of architectural engineering. I design the engineering of the "bones" of a building—the part of the structure that keeps you safe in a hurricane, an earthquake, or a blizzard. Many of the projects I have worked on contribute to a better world through lower energy usage and sustainable design. I've been blessed to design numerous projects that help people, such as hospitals, schools, labs, and university buildings.

I am also extremely frustrated and angry with the status of women in engineering today. Loving what you do while being equal parts dismayed is a difficult place to be.

I am angry because recent headlines indicate a wave of abhorrent behavior largely perpetuated by men against women. An Internet search of "female engineer sexual harassment" found 3.57 million results. Headlines in recent months include "Women in Tech Speak Frankly on Culture of Harassment" (*The New York Times*), "Sexual Harassment in Tech: Women Tell Their Stories" (CNN) and "Yes, Sexual Harassment in Tech is really that bad, 78% of Female Founders Say" (Inc.).

I am frustrated because in contrast, if you were to ask ten working female engineers—in mixed company, and particularly those working in non-computer engineering fields *outside* of Silicon Valley—if their gender had any bearing on their careers, eight of them would supply a vague, politically correct response: "I'm working to be the best engineer I can be," or maybe, "Gender does not play into it."

Ask the same question in a room of *all-female* engineers, and a different picture emerges. This picture is of women who have not experienced harassment, but are instead struggling with feelings of isolation and frustration with being asked to do non-engineering tasks such as taking notes while the male members of their teams do the engineering. They see themselves being left out of informal interactions crucial for career growth that their male counterparts receive. They are frustrated and exhausted. They feel they have to work twice as hard as their male engineering coworkers to be taken seriously.

How do these women respond? Some engineers leave for other fields. If you are like me, however, quitting is not in your DNA. You commit to working harder. You put your head down, work harder, and make a focused effort to "fit in" with the guys. You develop a thick skin and laugh off sexist remarks.

A year or more later, you look back—as I did— and realize that all that hard work and attempts to fit in haven't made much of a difference. This was me. I thought that acting more like the men, working harder, doing what everyone else was doing, and making sure I knew all the correct technical answers were the requirements for engineering success. Instead, I felt stuck in my career and exhausted, trying to keep up. Working harder wasn't working for me. And while I suspected that gender bias could be contributing to my frustrations, I had an uncomfortable feeling that bias alone was not the culprit.

Not sure how to move my career forward, I did what I have always done when stuck—I did research, embarking on a multi-year journey of reading, talking to other female engineers, learning from other industries, testing the techniques I uncovered, and learning through trial and error. That journey is far from over, but in the process I found the keys to success as a female engineer, the keys that neutralize gender bias, silence critics (including that nagging inner doubter), accelerate your earning potential, and allow you to have a life outside of work.

I want to give you the keys to the kingdom so you too can have engineering career success. Your success will come in part because you are a woman, not in spite of it. More importantly, the keys give you the knowledge and the resources to help you develop and achieve YOUR specific career and life goals, not someone else's vision (or lack thereof) for your path.

"She Engineers" was written to give you the keys.

Studying and applying the keys in this book result in higher earnings, promotions, and career satisfaction. You will become the leader you are meant to be. You will be a role model to other women. You will gain influence. You will become a force to be reckoned with in your chosen engineering field. And you can do this without leaving part of yourself at home so you can "fit-in" with the men at work.

The alternative is to waste years of frustration as I did trying to figure out why you aren't achieving the success you deserve.

I know these keys work because I have lived them. I am a female structural engineer who has worked for fifteen years as an engineering design consultant in the building industry for both large and small firms in the south and the northeast United States. I have managed the structural design process of large, complex engineering building projects totaling more than $500 million in construction costs to date. I have more than doubled my salary since I started working, and have been promoted twice in the time I have been with my current employer, including a 12% raise in the last two years alone. I am the chair of a national structural engineering committee in my field, the first-ever female chair (and youngest) of this particular committee.

During this same time, I've started a family. My girls are nine, six, and three at the time of publishing this book. I took short (unpaid) maternity leaves for each one before returning to work. We are a two-career household, and we don't have a nanny or a housekeeper. Our Toyota has almost 200,000 miles on it, and the house we purchased was a foreclosure that we have been fixing up. I enjoyed the city life early in my career, but decided to move to a small college town for the more relaxed lifestyle while still working on the engineering projects I love. I tell you all of this so you know I can relate to the everyday struggles and experiences of your life. I also want you to understand that, like me, you can live and work where you choose, and enjoy a satisfying engineering career and family too!

Which brings us to the inspiration behind writing this book.

In 2016, I attended two industry conferences. One was technical, and one was an engineering leadership conference. During each conference, I found myself in a group of women having this discussion: "So what is it *really* like to be a female engineer?" Many of the women talked about developing a thick skin, learning to brush off sexist comments, and trying to act like "one of the guys." Very often I was the only one in the group with one young child—let alone more than one. Very often I was greeted with surprise when my children came up, and I was asked to explain how it was possible to have multiple small children while working as an engineer.

My oldest daughter is nine, and she is showing an interest in engineering. She thinks the 3D engineering analysis models I build on the computer as part of my job are cool, and she is very proud of what I build. She even googled me at school one day to show her friends. If she chooses to be an engineer when she is older, I want her—and all the girls in the world like her—to have this book as a guide to navigate her career. I don't want her to waste years of effort working hard on the wrong things and not being rewarded for her work.

So I invite you into my family. I will share with you the stories, resources, and advice I would share with my daughters to prepare them for entering the engineering profession. I will show you the keys to become a successful female engineer. I will use the same "don't beat around the bush" and "tell it like it is" language we use at home. Everything I will tell you is true in my experience and research, and has been organized into a framework that you can apply immediately.

Are you a woman thinking about embarking on a career in engineering? This book will help you decide if you are prepared for the rigors of being in a highly technical, male-dominated field. It includes all the straight talk I wish someone had told me while I was selecting a major, along with tips on activities and electives that will accelerate your career progression from the day you start working.

Are you an early or mid-career professional who is feeling stuck and frustrated in your career progression? This book will teach you how to break through your current stagnation with actionable tools tailored to female engineers. The standard career progression advice given to male engineers doesn't work in the same way (and in some cases could backfire!) when applied to women. Avoid those traps by reading on.

Do you feel like you are working hard and getting nowhere? I've been there. This book will break you out of this rut.

Do you either have kids currently or want a family in the future? Chapter 8 is for you. We discuss the uncomfortable topics no one wants to bring up in a male-dominated work environment: maternity leave, breast pumps, and the critical importance of a support system when you have kids.

Do you work with, mentor, or manage female engineers? This book will give you valuable insights to better understand and more effectively work with female engineers and to build a stronger team. Studies show that a team split evenly along gender lines (as opposed to all-male or all-female) increases profits by 41 percent.[1]

Sadly, a large amount of frustrated and angry female engineers leave the industry. Of graduating engineering majors, only 20 percent are female,[2] and of those, 40 percent drop out or never enter the industry. Worse, one in four women leave engineering after age thirty while only one in ten men do the same.[3]

I don't want my daughters (should they choose to become engineers) to be a statistic. I don't want YOU to be a statistic.

Read this book now to avoid becoming that statistic. Don't be a member (as I was) of the sisterhood of frustrated female engineers. Don't spend years of your life working harder without achieving the success you deserve. It's all in this book. All you need to do is read on and apply the lessons I've learned the hard way.

Be the female engineer you are meant to be. Be the one that other engineers—male and female—emulate because of your ability to lead, to exude grace under pressure, and to maintain your own identity in the face of challenges. Be the role model your current or future children, nieces, and nephews can look up to. Chart your own path.

How to use this book

How can you use this book to chart your career path? Each chapter covers a key skill necessary for career success. Each skill is illustrated using current research, statistics, stories, and examples of how to use these skills. Each chapter concludes with a "Career Acceleration Challenge," three specific actions you can take immediately to apply the skills and start creating the career of your dreams. Most actions are designed to be completed in thirty minutes or less.

Although you might be tempted to pick and choose chapters that look particularly applicable to your life right now, I designed the book to be read and studied in chronological order for maximum benefit.

Chapter 1 teaches you how to find your own strengths and apply them to develop a leader's mindset and strategy. You will imagine what success looks like for you, and learn secrets to achievement as a woman in a male-dominated field.

In Chapter 2 you will learn how to become an engineering expert so that you have the leverage to achieve the success you defined in Chapter 1.

Chapters 3 and 4 show you how to demonstrate your engineering expertise to others through mastery of communication skills. You will learn which communication skills are most critical to engineering success and how to develop these skills quickly so you that can earn promotions, make more money, and have your pick of the best engineering projects where you work.

In Chapter 5 you will apply the skills learned earlier in the book in high-stakes situations to elevate your career to the next level. You will learn how to make networking work for you, even if you are an introvert (like me) and hate talking to strangers. You will learn how to stand out as a woman in a positive way so that you can be yourself at work.

Chapter 6 is all about finding your dream job. It flips standard job-hunting advice on its head, and shows you how to find an engineering position that is perfect for you. You will learn how to maximize your satisfaction at work, and why working harder doesn't really work.

In Chapter 7 you will learn the facts and myths surrounding gender bias and women in the engineering workforce. You will discover how to avoid gender-based pitfalls and neutralize bias in a way that does not result in ostracizing yourself from your workplace. You will learn the single most critical thing you can do for career success.

Chapter 8 shows you how to have a life outside of work as a female engineer. If you have or someday want children, you will learn tools I have used to integrate career with family. I also address being pregnant in an office of men and how to minimize the gender wage gap in this chapter.

This book will teach you how to be the best female engineer you can be, but only if you read it, study it, and apply what you will learn. It will empower you to use your natural strengths to create an impactful, well-paid engineering career. It will show you how to conquer bias, kick your inner critic to the curb, and create the career of your dreams.

Ready to change your life and enjoy an engineering career on YOUR terms? Let's get started!

A note for male readers

Most male engineers are just as appalled as their female counterparts by instances of sexual harassment and gender bias. Many of them have wives and daughters who are engineers and are personally invested in helping female engineers succeed. These strong men celebrate the rise of the smart, confident, successful female engineer. I should know, as I am married to such a man.

While *She Engineers* was written for female engineers by a female engineer, men will find many useful tools throughout that they can apply to their own careers. This book is not intended to bash men—quite the contrary, in fact. Since you picked up this book, you understand that we all benefit from perspectives different than our own. You know that diverse teams are more innovative and profitable than their counterparts.

But, just as I can't fully comprehend the male mind, you may not know what to do to help your female colleagues succeed. Particularly if you are managing a team with women, you may be wondering why the advice that you've given to male engineers just doesn't seem to work for the women. This book will change your perspective and give you new tools to create higher- performing teams.

Chapter 1

WHO ARE YOU?

ENGINEERING YOUR MIND

Welcome to the female engineer tribe! Whether you are just thinking about a career in engineering or have been working in the field for years, this book is for you. Engineers are smart, problem-solving, creative individuals. We are the elite teams of modern society, creating everything from smartphones and modern medical advances to buildings and clean drinking water. We have a significant impact on the world.

As with any team, we must know the players' capabilities to understand what position they need to play. Would you play a defensive lineman as quarterback on a football team? I thought not; however, the team needs them both. They have unique skills that are necessary for the collective team to succeed. Put the wrong person in the wrong position, and chaos ensues. The team can't reach its maximum potential.

Like the quarterback or lineman, you have unique skills and assets, some of which you may be aware of while others may be hidden for the moment. We will coax those skills from their hiding places as we learn how to turbocharge your engineering career.

How you choose to use your skills determine the two choices that await. Do you want to be a leader or a follower? What's the difference? A follower allows others to define her path and tell her what to do. A follower's path follows the status quo and travels to a destination others have chosen for her.

A leader, in contrast, knows herself well. She gives herself the opportunity to learn, grow, and develop the best parts of herself. In turn, this growth allows her to become the best engineer she can be. She creates her own vision and a career path of her own choosing. She defines success on her terms, and she uses her strengths to place herself in the best position—for her!—on the team.

Do you want to lead or follow? If you are reading this book, I'm going to assume that, like me, you want to lead. And like me just a few years ago, you may feel overwhelmed and not know where to start. This book will show you the simple strategies that have allowed me and countless women like me to unleash their inner leaders. They will work for you too.

In this chapter, I will teach you the leader's mindset and strategy. You will learn your strengths and values. You will define your success, and you will learn the secrets to becoming a successful female engineer.

Know yourself

You can't achieve success in your life if you don't know yourself well. You are unique. You are smart. Do not try to fit yourself into what you may perceive as the "ideal engineer" mold.

Even among engineering fields, the concept of the ideal engineer varies. For a computer engineer, we imagine the T-shirt and hoodie uniform of Mark Zuckerberg. In my field—the consulting arm of the architecture, engineering, and construction industry—it's a khaki-wearing, hard-hat-toting older gentleman who may also have a deep desire for a low golf handicap.

The desire to conform is a very natural instinct from an evolutionary standpoint, but when our desire to fit in begins to overcome our sense of self, it is easy to start doubting ourselves. It is easy to start thinking that since we don't look like an ideal engineer, we can't become as good (or better!) as someone who does.

That thought is called a limiting belief. We all have limiting beliefs, but many of us are unaware of them.

Think about your childhood for a minute. Were you raised to challenge authority, be courageous, and try new things? Were you taught to take care of those around you, avoid conflict, and please others? American society typically encourages the first set of behaviors for male children, while the second set is preferred for a female child.

Now think about how this applies to your work environment and how it shapes your psyche and those around you. Are the women around you encouraged to be people-pleasing, agreeable, and "punished" if they rock the boat or are vocal in disagreements? For example, in an all-hands office meeting, my manager once instructed me to "be cooperative" when dealing with a particularly challenging client. What did my manager say to a man in a similar situation? "That is just a difficult client—thanks for straightening them out."

As a female engineer, a lot of colleagues, managers, bosses, and even clients will try to pigeonhole you based on their own limiting beliefs and expectations. Don't be the female engineer that takes this personally, which is what I did in my early years. That results in carrying around a chip on your shoulder that limits your effectiveness.

When this happens to you, remember these two things: (1) They are simply projecting their own beliefs onto you. (2) It is not your responsibility to conform to others' limiting beliefs; your responsibility is to be your best self.

Knowing yourself is the first step. Aligning your outer world (for example, work) with your inner world's core values is how we put this all together.

Let's start with personalities, specifically the introvert versus the extrovert. Our ideal engineer stereotype is the introverted geek who is married to his computer and who has no social life. At the opposite end of the spectrum, American society encourages and values the extroverted personality—the life of the party, the caring mom, the gregarious politician. These are the personalities featured on news and social media.

Are you an introvert or an extrovert? If you're not sure, think about how you relax. At the end of a particularly long day, do you want to be alone with a good book, TV show, or video game, or would you prefer to go out with friends? Needing alone time to recharge is a classic sign of an introvert while extroverts generally prefer social time to recharge. If you are like me and most of the engineers I know, you have introverted tendencies.

Why does this matter?

This key personality trait is just a small part of who you are, but it matters because women who are introverted engineers are bucking multiple societal expectations. In contrast, men who are introverted engineers are "forgiven" by society because their eccentricity is chalked up to their brilliance. People make excuses for these extremely intelligent men who lack certain social and people skills, and it's not hard to find them grouping together in industries such as tech.

An introverted woman, on the other hand, is perceived as cold: she must not be caring if she prefers not to be around people all the time, or she's weird instead of brilliant. Society expects a woman to be social and "punishes" her accordingly if she is not.

This personality trait also matters because extroverts and introverts create relationships differently. Extroverts tend to have many acquaintances while introverts typically experience deeper relationships with just a few close friends. We'll talk more about how you can use your personality type to your advantage when networking in Chapter 5.

You should consider different engineering career paths based on your personality type. For example, if continuous interaction with others exhausts you, then you will want to select a more technical role in which you will be spending a good portion of your day on tasks you can complete independently. If you are extroverted, you may prefer a business development role that allows you to combine both your technical interests and your desire to interact with others.

Determine the tasks you most enjoy and figure out how to apply them to your career. The first step in this determination is to define your personal values.

Do you know what you value? One of my core values is also one of the reasons I am writing this book. This value is honesty. It is my hope that by using this core value, I will help other female engineers rise to the top of their fields.

Perhaps you are not sure what you value. If this is you, consider the following:

o   Where do you spend the vast majority of your time and money?

o   What do you love to do when you are working?

o   Ask three of your closest friends how they would describe you. You'll likely see some similar trends in their responses that you can translate into values.

Now, write down your top three values.

My values

1.

2.

3.

Picking a career path that aligns with these top values is crucial to your life and work success. For example, let's say you have always hated seeing brand-new, sterile-looking subdivisions go up, but you have always loved home renovation shows on HGTV. That means you are unlikely to be happy working for a civil engineering firm that specializes in new subdivision development. On the other hand, you would be happy working for a developer that specializes in reuse and rehabilitation projects.

Now that you are more aware of your values, let's talk about your strengths. What do you love to do? In what subjects do your coworkers or friends come to you for advice? Is there something that comes easily to you that makes you unique in your social or work circles? Take a moment and write those down.

My strengths:

1.

2.

3.

I have known a number of engineers—both male and female—who have spent a lot of time shoring up weaknesses. Why? Engineers like to be precise. We like to be right all the time. We automatically argue with someone who does not agree with our point of view. We will argue on technicalities. The logical progression is to then to study and improve ourselves where we are weak so no one can prove us wrong.

In a quest to always be the smartest person in the room, I have seen engineers spend hours researching one topic that doesn't really interest them just to prove they are right. Unless you are really fascinated by the subject and are planning to become an expert in it, this is a waste of time. Focusing on your strengths puts you miles ahead of most engineers who exhaust themselves with all the things they need to "fix" about themselves.

Take the time to figure out the few things at which you really excel. Notice the one or two things that come easy to you and master those one or two things. Resist the urge to become acceptable at a lot of things, but a master of none. When you find your strengths, work no longer feels like work, and people will flock to you enthusiastically because of your knowledge of and passion for the material.

Your Values + Your Strengths = Success on Your Terms!

Define your own success

"Winners are not afraid of losing. But losers are. Failure is part of the process of success. People who avoid failure also avoid success." — Robert T. Kiyosaki, founder of Rich Dad Company, and author of "Rich Dad Poor Dad".

Now that you better understand your own values and strengths, let's figure out what your ideal career looks like. If money is no object, how do you spend your days? Are you working? Traveling? Playing? Does your life better align with both your values and strengths?

At this point you may be wondering if you purchased the wrong book. You may wonder why we are learning about psychology instead of engineering. You bought the right book. Stay with me because I'm about to teach you the secret to engineering success.

What is the number one thing that holds you back from success? It's YOU.

I've been there—I've held myself back. In college, I found myself thinking, "I don't know what I want to do," as I switched college majors for the third time. I never sat down to figure out my values and strengths. Instead, I waited until I got my first performance review to let others define those for me. Big mistake.

Why? Because by then I had "learned" that the "proper" career ladder (according to the corporate world) was to do what I was told and get promoted over time. I never thought to ask if that was what I wanted or needed. I never thought to ask if that was the best use of my strengths. I simply followed the herd.

Don't duplicate my mistakes.

Find your purpose. What were you put on this earth to do? Allow that purpose to define your priorities, and don't let anyone else define them for you. **You** are the only one responsible for your career path—not your boss or manager, your spouse, your family, or society. Choose intentionally.

How do YOU define success at work? Is it money? Prestige? Power? According to a recent Gallup Poll, for most people these don't even make the top three. Ron Friedman, PhD, author of *The Best Place to Work*,[4] and someone whom I've had the honor of hearing in a keynote at an engineering conference, says that the top three qualities people need to experience to enjoy their jobs are competence, relatedness, and autonomy. When employees experience these three qualities, they are engaged in their work. Engaged employees are more present, productive, and attuned to customer needs. Engagement translates into a 17 percent increase in productivity and a 21 percent higher profitability as compared to disengaged employees.

Your engagement at work is critical to obtaining superstar status at work.[5] Engagement requires being mindful of your purpose. It's also extremely profitable for both you and your employer.

Write down a few things you would find in your "ideal" work situation. Here are a couple of examples you could think about:

- o Two-way street of trust between myself and my customers, manager, and company

- o Flexibility to get work done when and where I see fit

- o Autonomy in how I get my work done

- o Work that has an impact on the world

- o Opportunities to write and speak on topics that interest me

- o Travel – Do you want to see the world or generally prefer to stay close to home?

- o Being surrounded by people with diverse interests and skill sets

Now write down a couple things you would find in your "ideal" personal life. Here are a couple of examples from my list:

- o Enough money to live a decent but not extravagant lifestyle, including enough to save for retirement and kids' college

- o A house owned free and clear

- o Work hours are reasonable (I don't want to routinely work 60+ hour work weeks)

- o Exercise daily

- o Have enough free time to catch up with friends over coffee or lunch at least once a week

- o Volunteer

- o Consistently get sufficient sleep (for me that is a solid 8 hours)

Look back at your lists, and pick three from each list that are most important to you. Next, consider how your current lifestyle reflects these priorities? **Are you expending the most time, energy, and money on the highest priorities?** Is there a balance between work and play?

The healthiest, happiest, and most successful engineers create a balance that is personally satisfying for them, a balance that directly aligns with their priorities. Remember, you are the only person who can define those priorities. Allowing others to define them for you— or worse, failing to define them at all—will result in a mediocre, unhappy career. Your success depends on the alignment of your personal priorities with your work. I want you to be happy. So, if you have been reading this and thinking to yourself you will do these exercises at some other time, STOP! Go back **now** take the time to complete these exercises before moving to the next section.

Secrets to success

There are four secrets to success as a female engineer. You must know yourself, be positive, take care of your own well-being, and give. Ignore any one of these secrets at your own peril. You may be surprised to see that these secrets do not specifically involve technical engineering knowledge. This is the biggest secret of all for career success—your success has more to do with your *internal* mindset than it does with your *external* knowledge. You can have plenty of external knowledge and be a mediocre engineer if your internal world is not in order. But if you cultivate the proper internal mindset, your ability to learn and apply external knowledge expands infinitely.

Secret 1 – Know yourself

Why do you need to know yourself? So you can define your own success. For some women this is a big paycheck, while for others it may be the freedom to work when and where you please. You need to accept that, due to the scarcity of female engineers, you will always stand out. This is true even if you try to become "one of the boys." You are going to be memorable simply because you are a woman. I will teach you later in this book how to use that to your advantage, particularly when networking.

I sucked at this one for a long time and still struggle with it at times. I was very much stuck in being a busy "doer" (the more the better!) without thinking about whether I was doing what was really important to ME in my life and career. I didn't learn to prioritize or delegate well, and it cost me a number of friendships. Don't be me. Know yourself. Once you do, use that knowledge to chart your path instead of letting outside forces chart it for you.

Secret 2 – Think positive

Shit happens. Sometimes it is sexist and unfair. Sometimes you'll have a crappy boss. Sometimes life deals you a poor hand. Let's hope these are the exceptions in your otherwise awesome life! When challenges do arise, we have two choices: We can complain about our situation and be miserable, and drive our friends and loved ones away with pessimism and a "victim mentality" about the unfairness of life as an engineer/millennial/female (insert whatever your plight is here).

Alternately we can consider the best advice one of my mentors gave me—"The only person you can change is yourself"—and we can cultivate the habit of a positive attitude. This type of optimism does not mean that we see a perfect world full of rainbows and unicorns. On the contrary, it means we have a deep-seated belief that our individual behavior matters. Our mindset and behavior has the power to change not only our own life but the world.

Science backs this up. Numerous psychological studies prove that you are what you believe, and all of us perceive a certain reality. Do you think you can complete a challenging project? You are right. Think you can't? You are also right.

Each of us has the power to decide to be optimistic. Every morning you can wake up and decide that today will be a good day by surrounding yourself with positive people and creating empowering habits in your life. We can choose to be in the driver's seat of our life (and if not us, who?), or we can choose to be a victim of circumstance. Optimism is required if we want to become an influencer (more on that in chapters 3 and 4). Which one will you choose?

Optimism is required for maximum engagement both at work and in life. It is even contagious to others. Don't believe me? Consider the scientific evidence:

1. Dr. Seligman at Penn compared salespeople's optimism scores to their performance. He did this across different industries, such as insurance, office products, real estate, banking, and car sales. The results from all the studies indicated that optimists outsold pessimists by 20 to 40 percent. His results from this and an earlier study were so definitive that he convinced MetLife Insurance to only hire people with high levels of optimism as measured by a test.

The results were amazing: those who scored in the top 10 percent for optimism sold 88 percent more than those ranked in the most pessimistic 10 percent.[6] (Spoiler alert: It is a myth that as an engineer you are not selling something. More on this in Chapter 5.)

2. Watching three minutes of negative news in the morning before work has been correlated with a 27 percent greater likelihood of reporting your day as unhappy six to eight hours later, as compared to others in a control group who watched positive or motivational news stories.[7] That quick break at work you took to check out cnn.com? If you read anything negative (and let's face it—most of it is negative!), this correlates with your unhappiness *hours* later.

3. B.L. Fredrickson's research shows that positive emotions broaden your attention and thinking, causing you to be able to make bigger connections and have more ideas. Her research shows this increases your cognitive function and results in substantial growth over time. Negative emotions, on the other hand, were shown to narrow your focus. That narrowed focus makes it harder to ward off everything from a cold to stress.[8]

4. Economically flourishing corporate teams have been shown to have a minimum ratio of 2.9:1 positive to negative statements during business meetings.[9] More on this in Chapter 3.

Engineers are natural problem solvers. Unfortunately, that also makes it is easy to slip into a habit of dissecting others' errors (supposedly so they won't be repeated). Let's be honest here: How does it make you feel when you have an interaction with someone who usually finds fault with your work? How likely are you to ask this person for help or to trust that person if you have a question?

Decide to be a solutions person. A team member screwed up? Don't assign blame; help the team find a solution. In doing so, you will build your reputation as someone who can be trusted when things go wrong, which is a critical leadership characteristic you will learn in Chapter 3.

For those of us who are not natural optimists, the good news is that we can become more optimistic with practice. Numerous studies have shown that cultivating gratitude is one of the fastest ways to increase your optimism. Start saying thank-you more often. Think of one thing every morning for which you are thankful.

In my house, we incorporate this idea in our family by telling each other one thing every evening for which we are thankful. It doesn't have to be something big—one child said she was thankful for getting a piece of candy for dessert. I was thankful we saw the sun today (November in the Pennsylvania mountains can be very gray).

You can also try a "complaining" challenge. Try not to complain for one entire day! It is much more difficult than you would imagine.

Thinking positively cultivates confidence, which is very strongly correlated with success and the "presence" needed to reach an executive level in your career (more on this in Chapter 4). Let's do a quick confidence check: If you have a hard problem that you can't figure out, what do you do? Give up and determine you just don't have the smarts to figure it out? Or do you keep working at it, researching it, and looking for more resources until you figure out a solution?

If you chose the second option, you have a growth mindset. If you chose the first, you have a fixed mindset. Too often these mindsets are correlated with gender. Let me explain.

Men are typically raised with a growth mindset. They may have an ingrained belief that they can learn anything if they practice often enough. A growth mindset means you can always learn something new. You believe your intelligence and skills are not fixed, but instead learned with practice. A fixed mindset, on the other hand, is much more predominant in women. You believe that your intelligence and skills are fixed.

As a child, were you rewarded for being smart, pretty, and well-behaved? This is a fixed mindset and fairly typical for how female children are raised in the United States. Alternately, were you taught that working hard, trying new things, and not giving up are valued? This is a growth mindset and is much more typical for how male children are raised.

If you have a fixed mindset, you can start small with some confidence boosters, such as trying new things with a high likelihood of success. This can include the volunteering we will discuss later in this chapter, the action items in Chapter 2 for building your technical expertise, or expanding your communication skills as discussed in Chapters 3 and 4.

However, I suspect you already have at least a partial growth mindset. If you are reading this book, you recognize that you can learn the skills you need to succeed. That you have chosen to maximize your career potential through this book proves you have a growth mindset. Congratulations and read on!

Secret 3 – Prioritize self-care

Secret 3 may be the most important section of the book. Everything else in this book is useless if you don't apply this section. Following it will lead you to raises, promotions, and the ability to achieve more than you ever thought possible!

The secret? Taking care of yourself by following the three keys of wellness: sleep, fuel, and exercise.

I understand that it's easier to say "yes" to happy hour than to the gym after work. It's easier to stay up late to finish a project, which results in us choosing "snooze" the next morning instead of the gym and consuming a delicious, sugary, caffeinated drink in the afternoon. The uniquely American culture of "do more" encourages us to stay up late to get that one last thing done.

The idea that taking care of yourself is directly correlated to your career advancement is a tall promise, and it may be an uncomfortable truth for many. You may even be rolling your eyes at me now. I ask that you bear with me for a moment as I tell a personal story that led me to this conviction, followed by the now significant body of scientific research that supports it.

I graduated college slightly overweight (180 on my five-foot-eight frame), and I dedicated myself to work and an active social life. I also never turned down the delicious foods and oversized portions in the southern city to which I moved, always rationalizing that I was working so hard I deserved those treats. Fast-forward three years, and I had gained fifty pounds. I knew I was overweight, but I still considered myself active (at least for an office worker).

We relocated to the Northeast, and a few years later, I had two children and I weighed almost 240 pounds. I was always exhausted and trying to figure out where my mojo had gone. My youngest child was now two, and I could no longer attribute it to sleep-deprivation. I was in my early thirties, so age could not be the reason either.

Then I saw a picture of myself, and I realized just how much weight I had gained. I determined that if I wanted to have healthy kids, I was going to have to set a better example. My daily intake of four Diet Cokes was going to have to change.

I started small. We already had an elliptical collecting dust, but I find running in place extremely boring. To make exercising less tedious, I decided that every night, as soon as the kids were in bed, I would get on the elliptical and "run" for thirty minutes while reading a book and listening to a motivating workout playlist. I also made "deals" with myself: I had to start, but if I was too tired to finish after fifteen minutes I could stop. Funny thing was, that rarely—if ever—happened.

I also decided to "eat healthier." For me, that meant portion control. Either oatmeal or a prepackaged turkey breakfast sandwich for breakfast, yogurt for a snack, and a Lean Cuisine or Healthy Choice for lunch. Dinner most evenings consisted of protein, vegetables, and starch. Little by little, the weight came off, and one year later I was down to 180. Two years later, I was down to 140 and had added running, weight lifting, and some yoga to my routine. I've maintained it on and off for four years and even had a third pregnancy during that time.

Are you wondering why I included my weight-loss story in a book about engineering? Well, the interesting thing is that when I lost all the weight, it boosted my confidence. I was suddenly more willing to take on not only more stretch assignments at work but also some (albeit small) risks. It was almost as if I had come out of a brain fog. I had proved to myself I could get in shape and maintain a healthy weight.

I discovered I have more energy and feel as if I can tackle anything in the day ahead when I exercise first thing in the morning before work, so I make sure I do this when I have an important meeting or event that day. It seems to make it easier to deal with any demanding client egos or challenging tasks in a way that nothing else can. Don't take my word for it - try it and see how you feel. Exercise can be as simple as a lunchtime walk. No fancy equipment or expensive gym membership needed!

You can also incorporate movement into your daily activities. At work, consider holding a walking meeting. This works best with no more than four people. The late Steve Jobs used to do this, and Mark Zuckerberg still does. The movement increases productivity by decreasing distractions, and in a 2014 Stanford study was shown to increase creativity by as much as 60 percent.[10]

In addition to exercise, the way we fuel our brains with food is important to being productive. The brain uses 20 percent of our daily calories even though by weight it makes up only about 2 percent of our body. The brain functions optimally with about 25 grams of glucose circulating in the bloodstream,[11] which is the amount of glucose in a banana.

So my switch to eating smaller, more portion-controlled meals that consisted primarily of lean proteins, vegetables, and whole-grain carbs really did bring my brain out of a fog—especially in the afternoon "slump." The processed foods I previously ate made my brain instantly happy for the glucose, but it quickly crashed back into the fog since processed foods leave the bloodstream so quickly. Frankly, I did not realize how bad I was feeling until I changed my diet. Cravings went away as well as the afternoon slump.

Study upon study also backs up my personal experience regarding exercise and eating well. In a study recently published in the journal *Medicine & Science in Sports & Exercise*, pairs of identical twins were studied in their early thirties. Controlling for all other factors, they found that after three years of one twin being sedentary and the other engaging in regular exercise, the sedentary twin was showing insulin resistance (a precursor to diabetes) and had less endurance and more body fat. They also showed a decrease in the gray matter in their brains in the areas responsible for motor control and coordination.

In a recent *Time* magazine article, Mandy Oaklander writes of similar experiments done on mice that showed that exercise effectively reversed the aging process.[12] She writes, "If there were a drug that can do for human health everything that exercise can, it would likely be the most valuable pharmaceutical ever developed."

Exercise—or really, movement of any sort—increases your cognitive function by increasing your testosterone levels and lowering your cortisol. This is linked to remaining calm under pressure, a key leadership skill you will learn about in Chapter 3.

Another benefit of exercise is stress management. Exercise—particularly any sort of cardio—produces the "feel-good" hormones that lowers your stress hormones. My favorites are kickboxing and tennis, and I also occasionally enjoy hatha yoga, particularly at the end of the day. Meditation, breathing exercises, and listening to upbeat or inspirational music have served to be great "pick me ups" also, which brings us to the ultimate form of stress management—sleep.

Why do we need sleep? Sleep is the mechanism by which the body heals and remembers. If you learn something new during the day or met a new person, sleep is how the brain forms the neural pathways that will enable you to remember tomorrow what you learned today. Obviously, as an engineer it is crucial that we are able to recall critical details of our designs and the problems we are working to solve. The trouble is, more than a third of Americans do not get enough sleep, according to CDC research.

How much is enough, you might wonder? "Enough" is defined as seven or more hours per night. What happens to our bodies when we consistently get less sleep? With even just one night of less sleep, you may notice that you have trouble remembering things that happened yesterday, are irritable, lose willpower (especially when it comes to food), and may have trouble making decisions. Lack of sleep reduces your brain's ability to function, including its ability to remember, and it increases your cortisol levels. Remember that low cortisol levels help you remain calm in the face of stress and are necessary for those critical leadership skills we want to develop. A perpetual lack of sleep that raises your cortisol levels also limits your ability to be a leader and excel at work.

Secret 4 – You get what you give

In his book *Give and Take*,[13] Adam Grant shares his powerful research regarding who "gets ahead" in business. He divides people into three groups: givers, takers, and matchers. Givers tend to give people whatever help they can. There are a couple different types within the giver group that vary in selflessness levels. Takers are selfish and tend to be the ones that use others, burning bridges on their way to the top. Matchers will match what others give them. Across all industries, Grant found that givers were overrepresented at both the top and the bottom. Those at the bottom generally had trouble setting boundaries, and givers at the top were the most successful in their respective fields.

To emulate the most successful, you must approach your career with a "how can I serve you" attitude as opposed to a "what can you do for me" attitude. We are a self-centered society, so if you give a little (while maintaining appropriate boundaries), you will find you gain a lot. This may mean asking your coworkers or clients how you can help them, asking your boss what you can do to advance a company directive, or strategically volunteering to gain new skills. Get started today by doing a "five-minute favor" (as Grant refers to it in his book). Make an introduction, forward an interesting article to someone, or write a thank-you email.

Volunteering and giving back can turbocharge your career and provide a great opportunity to stretch your skills in a low-stress environment. Volunteer to do things you don't normally do day-to-day, but which are of interest. Are you interested in getting into a different technical (or nontechnical) area in your company? Ask if someone in that area could use your help for a small project. If you are highly technical most of the day, then honing your presentation, speaking, and writing skills will be valuable in the future. One way to do this is by serving on a technical committee for a national organization in your field. These committees often publish the engineering standards for your field and provide direct access to industry experts from whom you can learn. In my field, for example, the American Society of Civil Engineers reserves some committee positions specifically for younger engineers who are not yet experts but have interest in the code and standard work.

The key here is to continually learn new skills that can either expand or complement your technical knowledge. I strongly support strategic volunteering; for example, look for groups in which your clients tend to participate and become active in them. Being active in whatever you choose to do is critical; simply adding a group to your resume does not reap any of the benefits of volunteering.

Specific examples could include volunteering to serve on the board of trustees for a nonprofit. The people who sit on those boards tend to have varied networks, giving you access to movers and shakers in your local community whom you may not otherwise meet. Just make sure it is a cause you truly care about. If you are there with an agenda other than to support the organization, it will be obvious (no matter how subtle you think you are being). Volunteering like this can help you develop a variety of skills, including insight into financial operations, public speaking, and consensus building, to name a few. And don't be afraid to "try out" a couple groups to find the right fit for you.

I also highly encourage you to join a professional committee in your industry in an area that interests you. Let me share my personal story with you on how this has benefitted me.

I was working in a company in a highly technical, "project engineer"-type role. I enjoyed the technical aspects of the job, but I had tremendous interest in developing my skills in the business side of my industry. I also like people and have a tremendous fascination with stories and personal motivations. I decided to apply to join a business practices committee in a national structural engineering organization.

At the time, I had almost zero experience on the business side with my employer, but what I lacked in knowledge, I made up for in enthusiasm. I made sure my application demonstrated my interest, and I was thrilled to be accepted to that committee.

During the first committee conference call, a request was made for volunteers to help write a magazine article. In the awkward silence that followed this request, I volunteered. I've always loved to write (which other engineers generally viewed as an oddity), so it seemed a natural fit for me. I took on that project with a passion that had been missing from my "real work" for some time.

A year later, I was a published coauthor in a national engineering magazine based on the work I did with that committee. That small win gave me the confidence to volunteer to present the same work at a national engineering conference the following year. That first presentation gave me the confidence to proactively research subject matter and coordinate the committee's creation of presentations for engineering conferences for the next two years. Those presentations gave me the confidence to start expanding my networking skills, including running for a trustee position in a local non-profit.

That domino effect resulted in my becoming the first female chair of that committee. That committee work gave me more confidence to speak up at work and in meetings, and it propelled my project management skills to the next level. None of this would have happened had I not had the courage to volunteer in an area of interest for which I was not at all qualified.

Giving resulted in greater satisfaction at work and gave me the opportunity to the develop strengths of mine that were sitting dormant. Giving can do the same for you too.

Chapter 1 – What you learned

You now know the leader's mindset and strategy. You understand your strengths and weaknesses. You may have already started to think about how you can better play to those strengths and put yourself in the best position to achieve. This chapter showed you how to define success and start cultivating your own path. With these basic tools in place, it's time to learn how to develop your technical knowledge. In the next chapter, you will use the success mindset developed in this chapter to become an engineering expert.

Chapter 1 — Career acceleration challenge

1. Success Definition: Write down the answers to the following question: What does success look like for you? Think about what the "best day ever" looks like for you. Where do you live? What are you working on?

2. Well-being: Write down three specific actions that can be completed within 15 minutes or less that you can immediately take to improve your well-being. Examples include take a walk over lunch, mediate for 15 minutes daily, or write for 15 minutes in a gratitude journal. Select one of the three items start incorporating it into your daily routine immediately. Bonus points if you can incorporate all three!

3. Give: Research and write down three possible volunteer activities and who you would contact to get involved in each. No need to pick one yet! We will do this in Chapter 2.

Chapter 2

BECOMING THE
TECHNICAL EXPERT

Chapter 1 showed you how to develop the mindset of the successful engineer. In this chapter, I will teach you how to become an engineering expert. Why an expert? Because as an expert you have the freedom to achieve success on your terms. Experts have options. They are sought-after leaders. Experts can work for themselves. If they choose to work for others, they have leverage to negotiate top-level compensation and other perks, such as a flexible schedule. Experts can have their dream career on their own terms. Are you excited to learn how to be an expert so you can have maximum impact on the world while living your dream life? Then read on.

It's a myth that you need to work for a top-tier engineering company to become an expert, but if that's a myth, then how do engineers become experts? Expertise is earned through the three principles you will learn in this chapter: technical knowledge, communicating that knowledge to others, and continual learning.

Do you believe that vast technical knowledge in one area is the primary requirement to being viewed as an expert? I will debunk that myth and tell you what to do instead.

Do you believe that experts don't have moments (or weeks or months) of doubt? I will show you why you should expect to experience doubt and how to overcome it.

Does gender have anything to do with your technical expertise or career progression? I'll show you science-backed research and give you experience-backed tools to be both aware of and neutralize gender biases.

Perceptions of your technical expertise matter

Bethanye Blount, a veteran software engineer in a senior position for a tech company, was interviewing a job applicant. The applicant refused to give her the time of day, despite her senior title and the fact that the applicant knew she was a decision-maker in the hiring process. When she tried to steer the conversation towards job responsibilities and technical skills, the applicant "blew her off with a flippant comment." After the interview, she spoke with another top female in the firm who said the applicant treated her the same way.

Clearly the applicant was not going to be hired; however, they had a male coworker who needed practice conducting interviews, so they asked him to talk to the candidate. The *Atlantic* article which tells this story describes what happens next:

When the (male) coworker emerged, he had an odd look on his face. "I don't know what just happened," he said. "I went in there and told him I was new, and all he said was he was so glad I was there: 'Finally, somebody who knows what's going on!'"[14]

Competence refers not only to technical ability, but also how we are perceived by others in the field. Female engineers start at a disadvantage because of societal conditioning as to what the "ideal engineer" looks like, as discussed in Chapter 1. For example, you may have to overcome first impressions that you are the secretary. You may, like me, be asked to take notes or fetch coffee. As Blount found out firsthand, you may even have to "prove" yourself to someone you are considering hiring.

How can you establish technical competence? By using four simple tools for maximum achievement. Applying these tools to your career not only guarantees that you achieve expert status, but they will also make others want to help you achieve. This is because your success means they will succeed as well.

The four tools are cross-training, curiosity, asking for help, and obtaining certifications. Let me show you how to use them to become an expert.

Tool #1: Cross-training

Learn as many aspects of your industry as you can, including the basics of business, marketing, and sales, in addition to engineering. Know your primary customer base. Know what "pain" your work solves for your customer. Request to work in various departments, on different projects, and on different teams within the same firm. You will learn how all the pieces in your industry and firm interconnect.

The likelihood of becoming a top executive in your field increases exponentially with cross-training. One study of 459,000 management executives on LinkedIn found that cross-training within one role was equivalent to an additional three years of experience (in title/salary/ benefits). People who cross-trained in four or more roles within the same industry attained roles and salaries similar to those with an MBA—without the MBA price tag![15] If you want to become a top executive, cross-training will provide you with a depth of experience within your industry that is critical to your success.

Of particular importance is making sure you understand your customer. Engineers are expert problem solvers—but sometimes we solve the wrong problem!

Problems must be approached from your customer's mindset. It's hard to understand your industry if you have never talked to your customer. I am continuously surprised by the number of engineers who don't even know who their customers are! To understand your customer and their needs better, find one and ask a few questions such as these:

o Why have you purchased this product or service?

o What would make this product or service even better?

o What is your number one business challenge with this product or service? How can I help you with this?

Knowing your customer helps you verify that your work purpose and your inner purpose are aligned. As we discussed in Chapter 1, magic occurs when you make this happen. Work is no longer work! Instead, we are on a mission to fulfill our purpose. We are no longer "selling" our work; we are rallying others to our cause.

Tool #2: Curiosity

Curiosity is required for problem-solving, which is why it is the key tool in establishing competence. We need to understand the "why" of an engineering problem before we dive into the details. Engineers usually enjoy being in the weeds. We enjoy calculations and are very detail-oriented. How many times have you started working on a project, only to discover that hours have slipped away and you don't know where the time has gone? If you are anything like me, this is a very common occurrence.

However, consider this: what if you just focused all that time on answering the wrong question? You can't get those hours back. Do you have time to waste? I thought not. Asking the right questions—so that your energy can be focused on solving your customer's most pressing problems—is therefore key and will result in establishing yourself as an expert quickly.

In my field, a client will often ask a seemingly simple question. Most of the time, though, the question they ask is not the real question; it is simply a symptom of the real problem to be solved.

Let's say that someone trips in front of you. They notice blood on their back when they stand up, so they ask for a Band-Aid. They can't see their own back. All they know is that there is some blood and the pain is manageable. You, on the other hand, can see their back, and you know that they need to go to the hospital for stitches. Would you hand the person a Band-Aid or take them to the hospital? Too often engineers hand the person a Band-Aid.

Take a recent conversation I had with a building contractor. "Can we use a steel lintel instead of a concrete lintel?" I was asked. A lintel is a beam located above a door opening to hold up the wall above it.

I thought to myself for a moment. I did not have time to redesign the concrete beam I had already designed in steel. The original design was sufficient from a calculation standpoint. Plus, the wall above was concrete, which made the concrete lintel seem to make the most sense. Suspending judgment for the moment and wanting to understand why this request was being made, I responded, "Can you help me understand what is driving this question?"

The contractor went on to explain that if we used the steel lintel and shifted the location a couple of inches, it could save the client money because it would avoid installing shoring for the existing wall in order to install the lintel. It would also eliminate the time spent waiting for the concrete to cure—typically three to seven days, minimum—thus speeding up the construction schedule. He further explained that any extra cost for the steel would be less than the savings from a shorter schedule. Needless to say, I designed a steel solution.

Had I not chosen to ask and understand the "why" behind the question, a less desirable outcome may have occurred. The contractor and I might have argued, with me insisting that I was not redesigning anything, and the contractor insisting that a new design was needed. Both of us would have walked away from the interaction with less than positive feelings toward each other. Why do feelings matter? Because people hire engineers they like and trust. It's hard to forge a lasting relationship with a client if you don't take the time to understand their needs.

Curiosity also applies to internal clients like your immediate manager. If your manager answers some of your technical questions with responses like "this is how we've always done this" or "this is based on experience," make sure you ask for more information if you don't understand why. Ask to be directed to the evidence, even if it is experience. Say "Tell me more about your experience so that I can understand why we do it this way."

Someday soon you will be in a position where you will need to teach someone else how to do the same thing you are learning. If you plan to become a leader (and I know you do because you're reading this book!), teaching and mentoring will be a key part of your future responsibilities. If you don't understand the "why," how can you teach anyone else?

Don't feel you need to ask complicated questions. Stick with journalist-type questions—*who, what, where, when, why,* and *how*— followed by "tell me more." Resist the urge to ask a leading question that proves you are "right" or shows your intelligence.

In her book *Wired for Authenticity*,[16] Henna Inam, a successful ex-executive in a Fortune 500 company and founder of Transformational Leadership, Inc., explains why sticking with basic questions is important to understanding. She writes:

The shorter and dumber my question, the more I learned. What I discovered by asking dumb questions is that the person responding had to dig deep for answers. There was less imposing my own point of view. There was more I could learn about what was important to others and what motivated them.

Try asking the following "dumb" questions today:

o "Why does this matter?"

o "What does success look like?"

o "What are your expectations?"

Curiosity ultimately results in increasing not only your ability to learn and grow, but your ability to understand and influence others. By diving deeper into the reasons behind what you do and what your clients do, you allow innovative ideas to surface. Curiosity also allows others to be heard and understood. That results in building trust, which is a key component of success leaders as you will learn in Chapter 3.

Tool #3: Asking for help

The third tool is asking for help. We've all heard the adage "Ask and you shall receive," but many engineers are often hard-pressed to ask for help. We think we can handle it all. We think we need to prove ourselves. We may even believe that asking for assistance is sign a weakness.

In reality, however, asking for help has the opposite effect, a fact that has been proven by science so often that it has coined the term "the Ben Franklin effect."[17] The first person to document this phenomenon was—you guessed it—Benjamin Franklin. In his autobiography, he writes of how he made friends with a hater by asking him for the favor of lending him a rare book. Franklin writes that it was sent immediately and that he returned it a week later with a letter expressing his gratitude. The two went on to become lifelong friends.

Asking someone for a favor is a compliment, a way of showing admiration and respect to another person. When we ask someone for a favor, we are signaling that we consider them to have knowledge or skills that we don't have, which immediately raises their opinion of us and makes them more willing to help us. Think about it—when someone seeks you out for your opinion about a subject, how do you feel? Chances are you enjoy the admiration and like the person more for asking. Giving someone advice simply feels good, and that good feeling is associated with the person asked for the favor.

If you are like me, asking for help is difficult, so here are some ideas to help you over that hurdle:

- Ask a colleague if they can help you find a building code reference.

- Seek out the experts in your firm or industry, and ask them to share their expertise and knowledge with you.

- Ask coworkers to share their knowledge with you. This can be as easy as having lunch with your boss and asking them what advice they would have given to their younger selves.

o   Ask a coworker or manager how they would approach a problem that is stumping you.

The other type of help needed is actionable feedback. Asking for feedback can be especially difficult for women in male-dominated industries. Men tend to give and receive informal feedback constantly to each other. In a friendly, ribbing way, they will slap each other on the back and say things like, "Nice presentation, John," or "You really stuck your foot in it there." Women don't tend to give or receive feedback in the same way.

Both men and women may be afraid to give feedback to women because they are afraid of hurting the woman's feelings and the resulting emotions (such as crying). A 2016 "Women in the Workplace Survey" of 34,000 employees studying women's advancement to the C-suites found that women were 20 percent less likely than men to report having received necessary difficult feedback that could improve their performance. Of the managers surveyed, 43 percent reported that they did not give this feedback because they were concerned it would be perceived as mean or hurtful, and 16 percent were concerned about an emotional outburst.[18]

This means you will likely have to ask for feedback multiple times before you receive it, and when you do receive it, you must not take it personally. If you get defensive, the person giving you the feedback is unlikely to give you advice ever again. Remember, feedback is not a personal attack. It's simply a way to learn and grow. Feedback helps you better understand how others perceive you, and is absolutely critical to your long-term career advancement. There is usually a gap between how you perceive yourself and how others perceive you. Don't like how you are perceived? Change it. But you cannot change it if you are unaware of it.

Imagine that you are a professional basketball player. Would you ask your coach only once a year how to improve? Of course not. Do you think you would be a top athlete if you taught herself how to shoot, practiced your method all year, and then found out your technique (which is now a habit) was wrong months later in a review? That would be ridiculous. Yet, this is what many engineers do with feedback by only asking for it (and managers only giving it) during yearly performance reviews.

You may be thinking that you are only a junior engineer and it is someone else's responsibility to give you feedback. You may think that your manager should simply give you feedback when you need it. But in reality, this often does not happen because many engineers are uncomfortable giving or receiving feedback. The result is that if you don't take responsibility for asking for feedback, you may never become aware of what is holding you back in reaching engineering expert status.

How can we ask for feedback, especially if it is not freely given? Here are some sample scenarios illustrating how you can ask for immediate feedback:

1. You just finished a short presentation to the office. Ask the group, "Hey, I would really appreciate your feedback in how I can make this presentation better next time. Can you each tell me one thing that could be improved?"

2. You just answered a tough question in a client meeting with your boss present. As you and your boss are walking back to your cars (or down the hall back to your offices), ask your boss "How do you think that meeting went? Is there anything I can do next time to better respond to the questions?"

3. You are working on a team with multiple other engineers. You bump into one of them getting coffee one morning. Ask "Hey, I've been thinking about how I can improve and was wondering if I could get some quick advice. Is there anything I can do that would make it easier to work with me?" When they say, "No, everything's fine," chuckle and respond. "So, what you are saying is I am perfect, right? Somehow I don't think so. Surely, you can think of just one thing I can improve. I would really appreciate the feedback." Then be quiet until they give you some information.

Tool #4: Earn certifications

What certifications or licenses do experts in your field hold? Are there any cutting edge areas where you can earn a new certification? If you want to become an expert, you must earn the critical certifications in your field. The big one for many engineers is the professional engineer, also called a PE license.

Why earn this certification? Because that certification gives you options. And as we have discussed, becoming an expert is all about having many options open to you so you can have your dream career. In many engineering disciplines, my own included, a registered engineer must sign and seal final drawings and calculations. That means engineers with a PE license are typically paid more and are in higher demand than engineers without this certification.

In my field of structural engineering, a PE license is typically required to obtain the most senior positions. It is the gateway to managing younger engineers, becoming a respected mentor, presenting at most conferences, or becoming an entrepreneur if desired. It opens doors that are nailed shut otherwise. Further, since it is a norm in my industry, if an engineer is six years or more out of college and has not yet submitted the application to take the PE exam, questions will be asked.

I once interviewed for a position and was told that the reason I did not get it was because "we made the offer to someone with a PE." Earning your PE license will give you a leg up on others who may have the same level of experience but do not have the certification.

Complete the application to take the PE exam as soon as you are eligible. The paperwork required includes items such as references and a written explanation of all projects you have worked on and calculations you have personally completed. That paperwork takes time. You can start compiling these items as soon as you start working so that when you meet the minimum experience levels for your field (typically four years), you can submit your application to take the exam. Licensing requirements vary by state (there is no national standard), so you will need to review your individual state requirements.

A variety of engineering knowledge is needed to pass the exam. If, for example, you are doing the same types of engineering calculations and analysis in your third year of work that you were doing in your first, you may need to discuss working in other areas with your supervisor. This is assuming this option is available at your current employer. Alternately you will need to spend a lot of extra time studying in areas where you do not have experience. Remember the cross-training tool? Here is where you start to reap the rewards of cross-training your engineering expertise.

For me, I decided when I started working to get my PE license as quickly as possible. Specifically, I wanted to complete the initial certification before I considered having children. This is because studying for the PE is very time-consuming. The vast majority of people that don't put in the hours to study do not pass the exam the first time. I knew I would have difficulty studying once children were in the picture. That decision may not be for everyone, but it was the right one for me.

I was fortunate that I had a lot of broad experience covering most of the areas tested on the exam, but it still required a lot of studying. In 2017, pass rates for my exam were 68 percent for first-time takers and 44 percent for those who were taking the exam for the second time or more.[19] You can see the pass rates for your engineering discipline at www.ncees.org/engineering/pe.

Other certifications available are field- and interest-dependent. I am aware of engineers with certifications in everything from project management to sustainability.

Additional college degrees can also be helpful. Some engineering disciplines essentially require at least a master's degree. A master's degree is also required in many cases if you want to teach at the college level. An MBA can be helpful if you are interested in the business side of your industry.

I want to be clear regarding certifications. Completing certifications does **not** immediately grant you engineering expert status. Some certifications may not even garner you a pay raise. They are the gateway to being an expert. They are the gateway to more money, status, and possibilities. Without them, your ability to progress to the top of your industry will be sorely limited.

That's not to say there are not exceptions. The media loves to share stories of extremely successful college drop-outs (especially in fields such as computer engineering) that don't have any of the typical certifications. But, if you are like me, and you want to put yourself on the path to the career of your dreams as quickly as possible, you will find obtaining the certifications puts expert status in reach more quickly, easily, and with less risk than any other option available to you.

Put the tools together: find your niche

Finding your niche is where the four tools of cross-training, curiosity, asking for help, and obtaining certifications pay off. It is where your problem-solving skills meet your strengths, values, and interests.

Cross-training gives you the ability to learn about and try multiple areas in your field. An engineer just starting out usually doesn't know where she is going to fit best. That's OK! Use the *curiosity* tool while cross-training to find out more. Use the *ask for help* tool to garner advice and feedback along the way. Earn the *certifications* necessary to succeed in your engineering area of expertise.

How can you specifically put these tools into practice today? Look for work and volunteer activities that pique your interest. It could be helping someone develop technical manuals as an internal guide, creating a calculation spreadsheet others can also use, writing a company blog post, or helping the marketing department with a presentation. Distinguish yourself early as a go-to person in your firm for *something*; it makes you an invaluable employee and gives you leverage to obtain all those expert options we have been discussing.

Still struggling to find your niche, especially if you are a recent college graduate? "I don't know anything I could teach others," you may be thinking to yourself. You are wrong. Start with technology. Many new graduates are very comfortable with technology, while more experienced engineers may not be as up-to-date. As a younger engineer, you could put together some "how-to's" for everyone in the company or your department on how to solve an engineering challenge using a software package.

Next, you could join a technical committee that revolves around that technology. Remember, as my story in Chapter 1 showed, it's a myth that you must already be an expert to apply to join the various technical committees. If you are willing to put in the work and be an active, contributing member, you will find that many committees are appreciative of younger members who have enthusiasm and interest in their subject areas—even if you are not an expert yet.

As we discussed earlier, cross-training is crucial to becoming an expert because the more areas you are exposed to in your field, the more likely it is you will find that area where your competence and your "why" aligns. If your heart is not in it, your customers, coworkers, and boss will know it.

Competence + interest = success!

What makes a good engineer?

You are now on your way to becoming a technical expert! But did you know there are numerous nontechnical pitfalls that can hold you back from your maximum engineering potential?

Let's step back and ask the question: what makes a good engineer?

The answer will surprise you. There is a difference between what the public thinks makes a good engineer and the reality of what makes a good practicing engineer.

Ask some non-engineering friends what they think makes a good engineer. "An engineer is smart," you may hear. "They are really good at math. They are detail and process oriented." You may hear someone describe Bill Gates or Mark Zuckerberg. Another may describe engineers as "very technical with an analytical brain." You may hear that they make the world a better place.

However, if you ask those who hire engineers what makes them hire a particular engineer, a different picture emerges. This is what you might hear:

- o Technical competence

- o Innovative

- o Flexible – can adjust to new design ideas and concepts

- o Team player – able to collaborate with others

- o Understands my needs

- o Meets deadlines

- o Problem solver

- o Explains technical concepts well to me

- o Responds positively to constructive feedback

So, to be a successful engineer, you MUST be technically competent, but this is not all you need to be, no matter how much you love the technical aspect of the job. I certainly entered the field ignorant of the fact that much of an engineer's success is very dependent on nontechnical aspects. Perception and presentation matter to your technical success.

To be an expert you must be trusted, so how do you create trust? There is a saying that people don't remember what you say; they remember how you say it. If you say, "I am an excellent engineer?" in a quiet voice that ends with a question mark, others will question if you are competent. If you say, "I am an excellent engineer," in a confident, commanding tone, you are likely to be believed.

More importantly than what you say, though, is what you do. Being true to your word—for example, getting things done when you say you will—is the single-most important non-technical thing you can do in your career. This will help you build a reputation as a person of integrity and as someone who can be relied upon and trusted.

Start creating trust through perception awareness. To do this, it is important to know and remember that men and women can present things in the exact same way and yet be taken completely differently from each other. Psychologically we emulate those in leadership positions because we subconsciously believe that behaving similarly will enable us to obtain a similar position.

This behavior is called mirroring, and it works well for male engineers modeling other males in leadership positions. If you are a female engineer modeling the same male behavior, it will likely backfire for two reasons: (1) You will be seen as inauthentic (i.e., trying to be someone you are not), which is a fast track to not being trusted. (2) There are specific behaviors that are acceptable or even desirable in men that are not acceptable or desirable in women. For example, if a man yells, he is seen as "taking charge," but if a woman yells at work, she is being "emotional." In addition, "assertive" and "go-getter" behavior from a man may be seen as "pushy" or too aggressive for a female.

Part of how you are perceived is reflected in male and female communication styles. For example, men tend to treat "no" as "not yet," while women tend to treat "no" as "not ever." Women may also take pushback on their ideas as a personal rejection. It is critical to be aware of your own perception of the word "no." If you tend to take rejection personally, work to reframe the "no" as "not now" and the rejection as a rejection of the idea only, not of you as a person.

When presented with a problem, men will immediately want to solve it; however, a woman's problem-solving process often involves talking it out. The challenge here occurs when you are a female engineer managing men and you want to talk things out. In those situations, you may need to preface the conversation with "just thinking out loud" so that the junior engineer does not interpret every word out of your mouth as the direction in which he should proceed.

Leaders are decisive and able to make intelligent decisions with incomplete information. Women who often talk out their problems at work can be viewed as indecisive. This in turn limits their perceived leadership potential. Women can combat this by being up-front about the fact that they will make the final decision, but they feel it is imperative that all facts be gathered and input solicited from others so that the appropriate decision can be made.

Part of perception awareness is being aware of the correlation between competence and likeability. Men can generally get by—and advance—if they are competent or likeable, and those at the top have the potential to be perceived as both. Women must walk a fine line to be perceived as both competent and likeable. Decades of research by psychologists show these two qualities are inversely correlated for women.

Tom's rudeness can be excused because he is a brilliant engineer with "eccentricities," whereas Sally must be both competent and pleasant to work with. Paul may not be the smartest engineer in the world, but that is OK because he knows and gets along with everyone. But if Jane is your manager, she's either very likeable but incompetent, or she is cold-hearted yet smart. It's certainly not fair, but it represents a deep-seated societal bias that has the potential to hold many women back.

In Sheryl Sandberg's book *Lean In*,[20] she dedicates an entire chapter to the success-versus-likeability quandary and the decades of research that support the assertion of a woman's double bind. One of the most compelling stories she cites is research by Columbia University.

Two professors wrote up a case study about a real-life Silicon Valley entrepreneur named Heidi, describing her journey to become a successful venture capitalist. Her story talked about the traits—such as her networking skills and her go-getter personality—that made her successful. The professors had one group of students read her story with her real name and a second group read the same story with the name changed to Howard.

The students then rated Heidi and Howard on their accomplishments and likeability. On success, the students rated them equally. However, they liked Howard much more. Heidi was viewed as selfish and not the type of person you would want to hire or work for. For men, success and likeability are correlated; however, we like successful women less.[21]

The ideal-woman stereotype has traditionally been a caregiver, someone who selflessly gives to help others; she is sensitive with a strong sense of family and community; she does not self-promote and certainly does not tell others what to do. A successful woman is at odds with this stereotype, resulting in a nagging feeling (for most of us, if we are really honest with ourselves) that we aren't quite comfortable with her success.

In contrast, as a society we are comfortable with the "type A" male stereotype. Men have traditionally been the providers. It is socially acceptable for them to be ambitious and to spend hours away from home at work. They are typically esteemed when they exhibit decisive decision-making traits. A man who matches this stereotype is both liked and competent; however, a woman acting in the exact same way is seen as competent but not she is not liked. Put another way, if there are two or more competent women in an office, whoever is *least* likeable will tend to be viewed as the *most* competent. In contrast, men can be both.

Perhaps the most critical component of perception management is to do what you say you will do when you say you will do it. This is a particular challenge for women who are conditioned to people-please which can result in telling people what they want to hear. A lot of women, myself included, tend to set overly optimistic time tables to get things done. When they find themselves behind, they will either kill themselves to get it done or ask for a deadline extension. It takes only one or two missed deadlines for anyone—male or female—to lose others' trust, which leads to career stagnation.

Because that trust is virtually impossible to regain once it is lost, a good rule of thumb is to under-promise and over-deliver. Set appropriate boundaries and know your own limits. You always have the option to say "no." If you don't feel you can say "no" at work, you can go to your boss or manager and ask which project takes priority and/or which can be delegated to others.

We have talked about how you can build trust and credibility and the importance of being perceived as confident, but oftentimes we get in our own way and allow self-doubt to take over. Here enters "imposter syndrome."

One study of UK millennials found that a full 40 percent of female and 22 percent of male millennials reported feeling like an imposter. Another study in the *International Journal of Behavioral Sciences* reported that 70 percent of people studied have felt this way.[22] A third study showed that this is particularly prevalent among minority groups.[23] Anyone in a situation where they don't "fit in"—be it due to gender, race, sexual orientation, or interests—is more likely to experience imposter syndrome.

The phrase was coined in 1978 by psychotherapists Pauline Clance and Suzanne Imes when they found that many women with notable achievements also had high levels of self-doubt. Imposter syndrome is a feeling that you don't belong and don't deserve to be here. This happens to me all the time, and most often, it happens on a construction site. If you are a man trying to understand this concept, think about how you would feel walking into a nail salon or an OB/GYN office. Would you feel like you belong?

You are in good company if you have suffered from imposter syndrome. Many famous women and men have admitted to feeling like a fraud. You are joining the likes of award-winning novelist Maya Angelou, actress Kate Winslet, comedian Tina Fey, author John Steinbeck, and Facebook COO Sheryl Sandberg by acknowledging that you have faced this feeling. Curious as to where you land on the imposter-syndrome scale? See Pauline Clance's website for a free test, www.paulineroseclance.com/impostor _phenomenon.html.

Imposter syndrome is linked to perfectionism, a trait that tends to be more prevalent in women than men. Some even suggest that imposter syndrome is a prerequisite for greatness.[24] Studies suggest that high achievers are particularly prone to imposter syndrome because of the impossibly high expectations they set for themselves. Sound familiar?

Imposter syndrome has been presented in most forums as a self-confidence issue. However, having experienced the subtle "pushback" as a female in a male-dominated industry, I believe the loss of confidence results from a work environment that is inhospitable to workers who don't match the ideal stereotypes. A woman's confidence is undermined every time someone wants to know what she did to succeed (implying that is unusual); how she is balancing family and kids (that question NEVER gets asked of a man); how she will keep up that travel schedule when she has kids (assuming that she wants and can have kids); or what led her as a woman to become an engineer (once again, men aren't asked that question). After a while, even the most confident woman will begin to doubt her abilities.

In *Model View Culture*, a magazine about technology, culture, and diversity, author Cate Huston reflects on a similar experience in tech culture:

"What we call imposter syndrome often reflects the reality of an environment that tells marginalized groups that we shouldn't be confident, that our skills aren't enough, that we won't succeed—and when we do, our accomplishments won't even be attributed to us. Yet imposter syndrome is treated as a personal problem to be overcome, a *distortion* in processing rather than a realistic reflection of the hostility, discrimination, and stereotyping that pervades tech culture."[25]

The following are some practical tips to help you overcome imposter syndrome.

1. Name it. The next time you are in a situation where you feel awkward and as if you don't belong, say to yourself, "That's

just my imposter syndrome talking." Feelings don't hold as much fear if you can name them.

2. Prepare, prepare, prepare. When you are going into a situation that you are aware can trigger imposter syndrome be prepared by learning everything you can prior. If, for example, it is a meeting, ask for an advance agenda, who will attend the meeting, and if you are expected to make recommendations during the meeting.

3. Learn to trust yourself. I've watched some younger engineers struggle with speaking up in a group setting. I've also seen someone a month out of school ask a "dumb question" that resulting in saving a client thousands of dollars on a project. Can you guess which one was promoted more quickly? Your unique perspective is valuable regardless of experience level.

4. Ask questions if you don't know the answer. Use those "dumb" questions we talked about earlier in the book. Even the experts don't know all the answers. Take a cue from Dr. Chan, chief of the World Health Organization, who said "There are an awful lot of people out there who think I'm an expert. How do these people believe all this about me? I'm so much aware of all the things I don't know."[26]

The last component you need to know about perception management is related to risk. Engineering experts typically need to take risks in order to be successful in their careers. That can mean trying a new experimental technique. It can be leaving a comfortable position that isn't particularly challenging to start their own venture. Women are typically raised to be cautious in taking risks. That is a very good trait in most cases, as long as you continue to grow. Growth by its very nature requires pushing at the edges of your comfort zones. And pushing your comfort zone is absolutely required to become an expert.

How do you step out of your comfort zone? By trying new things and overcoming new challenges. Each challenge you overcome gives you a little more confidence to conquer the next challenge. To overcome new challenges, practice thinking positively, which leads to creative problem-solving. Always try to see the good things in a situation, and look for creative solutions rather than blaming someone or determining all the reasons something can't work.

Another way to step out of your comfort zone is to try new things that offer you the opportunity for fast failure in a relatively low-risk environment, such as a new hobby, running a marathon, or a volunteer opportunity. You will find the more you grow and challenge yourself (either in or out of the office), the more your confidence to conquer new challenges grows.

Growth not optional

The final key to becoming an expert in your field is to practice continual learning. We live in a society where everything is changing quickly. You can either grow, or you can stagnate and become obsolete. Engineers must constantly learn new things and be on the lookout for new technologies and innovations if they want to be leaders.

This is necessary for both technical and soft skills. Studies show engineers with strong communication and leadership abilities are in much higher demand than those with only technical competencies. We know that technical skills are required; however, if you can't explain your brilliance to nontechnical people (who are usually the ones with the money), all the engineering prowess in the world won't help. More on this in chapters 3 and 4.

Try one or more of the following eight practical, specific ways to grow in your abilities and cross-train at the same time:

1. Volunteer with a technical committee in your industry. This does so many things for you, including opening up your network and giving you access to other experts in your field.

2. Get additional certifications in your field, be they additional degrees or certificates. Some fields require a master's degree.

There are certifications for subset areas such as project management or sustainability. Many employers will even pay the costs for these programs.

3. Volunteer for stretch assignments at work. Did you know that men tend to overestimate their abilities while women tend to underestimate theirs? That means that if you see an interesting opportunity to try something at work, volunteer. Your male counterpart (who may be less qualified) thinks he can do it. Those assignments will help increase your knowledge and help you cross-train.

4. Request to work with multiple different senior engineers on projects so that you can observe different leadership styles and project types. Doing this will also enable you to observe which leadership styles work and which do not.

5. Ask for feedback from everyone on how you can improve.

6. Seek out innovators and industry experts. Read their blogs and ask them for advice for an aspiring engineering leader. Many are happy to share their knowledge.

7. Read. Become well-read in your industry and stay on top of the latest innovations and trends.

8. Talk to the marketing professionals, salespeople, and the IT people within your company. Learn how they sell your engineering products and how they enable or support your engineering function.

Secrets to success: finding a mentor

Imagine if you had a step-by-step roadmap to career success. How quickly would you achieve your goals? What would you do with the time saved? Nurturing a relationship with a mentor and a champion is your shortcut to create this roadmap. It is the most well-known, yet underutilized, secret to career success.

They are multiple people in your industry who have been where you are currently. They have faced the same challenges you are facing. They have solved those problems and learned lessons along the way. All you need to do is find them and follow in their footsteps. Find and cultivate a relationship with at least one mentor or champion.

What is the difference between these two roles? How can each help you?

A mentor is someone who acts as an advisor. A mentor provides guidance but usually does not actively advocate on your behalf. Mentors outside your current employer are valuable because they provide insight from a third-party perspective. Mentors inside your company are helpful because they often work directly with you and can offer actionable feedback because they better understand the specific situations and personalities involved.

A champion, on the other hand, is someone who acts both as an advisor and an advocate. Many champions start out as mentors. You turn a mentor into a champion when you provide assistance to them and they are impressed enough with your work to recommend you to others. A mentor can be requested, while a champion must be earned. A champion will bring up your name behind closed doors for promotions and projects. He or she will help propel your career more quickly to expert status.

A formal arrangement is not needed to start either a mentor or champion relationship. All you need for success is a relationship which meets the following two criteria:

1. The relationship is a two-way street. In chapter one, we talked about how we get what we give. As a young engineer, you must be willing to give something in return for the time your mentor or champion gives to you. You may provide assistance on a project at work or make an introduction at a networking event. At a loss for what you can do? Hand write a short, sincere thank you note to someone who has provided advice, telling them how this advice has or will help you.

2. The mentor or champion must be willing to give you honest feedback and suggestions for improvement. You, in return, must be willing to accept this feedback without taking offense and then act upon it. This means that when someone gives you negative feedback, you listen with the intent to understand. You do not become defensive by arguing or justifying the behavior being criticized. You thank the mentor or champion for being willing to give you feedback. You will learn more about how to actively listen and remain calm when receiving feedback in chapter three.

Excellent mentors and champions can be difficult to find. As a woman, the pool potentially shrinks further because mentors often tend to favor those who remind them of themselves when they were younger (which in most cases was not a woman). Mentees often show the same types of unconscious bias towards potential mentors. In addition, older men may be concerned about mentoring younger women because of the fear of being accused of impropriety. For an older man, attending happy hour or the golf course with a young male protégé does not raise eyebrows. The same activity with a young woman—unless she is in a group, in which case she won't receive the same benefits as the young male protégé would alone—is a different matter.

Be proactive in seeking out mentors. If your firm has a mentorship program, take advantage of the opportunity. If you work somewhere without a mentoring program, many engineering societies are now offering these programs which are typically free to join and a great place to make a connection. Still need help? Email me at stephanie@engineersrising.com.

Chapter 2 – What you learned

You are now on your way to becoming an expert. As an expert, you are constantly expanding your knowledge, sharing it with others, and seeking out continual learning and growth opportunities. You are aware of how you are perceived by others, and take steps to improve that perception. You may experience imposter syndrome but you don't let fear stop you. You know the importance of a mentor and champion and seek both out in a mutually beneficial relationship.

The next chapters break down each of these subjects individually, giving you the tools to elevate your expert status. Chapter 3 covers specific communication mindsets required of engineering leaders—with specific attention to female leaders—and how to develop them. Chapter 4 teaches you how to put the communication traits developed in Chapter 3 to work. Chapter 5 shows you how to use the technical expertise from Chapter 2, combined with the powerful communication mindsets and skills from Chapters 3 and 4, to become a powerful influencer. Chapter 7 teaches you how to find the right company and position for your unique values and aspirations. Chapters 8 and 9 give you the tools necessary to successfully navigate gender bias and having a life outside of your engineering career.

Chapter 2—Career acceleration challenge

1. Expert Interests: Write down three areas of your field where you have the greatest interest in becoming an expert. For each field, spent 10 minutes researching who is the current expert (or experts) in your field. Who are they and where do they work? What committees do they sit on?

2. Certifications: Write down the following:

   a. Three certifications you could obtain in your field.

   b. The results you expect if you obtain that certification. (More money? Promotion?)

   c. Circle the certification that has the best expected results according to your values.

   d. Complete one (15 minute or less) action that is the first step to achieving that certification. It could be research such as obtaining a graduate degree, or PE licensure requirements in your state.

3.   Volunteer: Join one organization of interest to volunteer. To complete this challenge, pull out your volunteer list from Chapter 1 and compare it to your answers to challenges 1 and 2 in Chapter 2. Do any of the volunteer areas you listed align with either of these categories? If so, select that area and immediately contact the organization to get more information and begin volunteering. If there is no alignment, that's OK. In this case, either a. add items to the volunteer list that do align and use that one to complete the challenge; b. pick the volunteer area that is most interesting to you and complete the challenge.

Chapter 3

LEADERS COMMUNICATE

Multiple studies show that we spend up to 80 percent of our waking hours involved in some method of communication. Broken down further, we spend 25 percent of our communication time writing and reading, 30 percent speaking, and 45 percent listening.

Study after study also shows most people—including engineers—need help in the communication department, and as we learned in Chapter 2, effective communication is a prerequisite for becoming a great engineer.

Engineers typically become engineers because they love the technical aspects of the field. Undergraduate engineering degree requirements focus predominately on the technical areas. The result is that most engineers never develop their communication skills beyond the most rudimentary trial-and-error approach. We then collectively wonder why no one will listen, why we are petrified of public speaking, and why we feel underappreciated.

Do you want to be the great engineer I know you can be? Do you want to be a shoo-in for promotions, raises, and the best projects? Are you currently—or do you want to become—a leader or perhaps an entrepreneur? Then you need to elevate your communication skills to the next level.

Leaders are communicators. In this chapter, you will learn the three most valuable traits (MVTs) needed to be an engineering leader. You will find out which communication skills are most valuable and how they can be developed so you can quickly achieve your goals. I will show you how to apply these skills in real-life situations for immediate impact at work. You will learn how to use your communication skills to become a best-in-class engineer.

Communication: what is it?

At 9:45 p.m. on April 20, 2010, a fiery explosion on the Deepwater Horizon oil rig killed eleven workers and injured seventeen more. One mile underwater, the oil well had blown apart, releasing oil into the Gulf of Mexico.[27] Oil would continue to flow for eighty-eight days. The well was owned by oil giant BP.

Tony Hayward, then CEO of BP, was a skilled geologist. As reported by *The New York Times* in April, in the early days of the disaster, Hayward told his fellow BP executives in frustration: "What the hell did we do to deserve this?" On May 13, he told reporters that the spill would be "relatively tiny." On May 18, Hayward told another news organization that the environmental impact of the spill "will be very, very modest."[28]

Shortly thereafter, stories began hitting the mainstream media about the economic disruptions that were resulting from the loss of fishing grounds and the extensive damage to marine habitats. At the same time, reports circulated of cleanup workers becoming ill because of the chemicals being used to disperse the oil.[29] The combined loss of tourism and fishing caused entire communities to lose their livelihoods because of the spill. On May 30, Hayward—a Briton— toured Louisiana to apologize for the spill. Instead, his now-infamous "I'd like my life back" comment was captured on video during that tour and went viral.

Public relations professionals have called BP's handling of the Deepwater Horizon disaster a classic case of PR gone wrong, but I think this story makes important points for engineers:

1. No matter how brilliant you may be technically, you can commit career suicide if you cannot communicate effectively.

2. Effective communication requires more than just opening your mouth and saying the first thing that comes to mind. It must be appropriate to the situation and audience.

All the technical prowess in the world means nothing if you cannot communicate it to others. The engineer who excels in communication will be perceived as the better candidate for the promotion almost every time, even if that person may have less technical capability than another candidate. Chapters 3 and 4 will give you the communication skills, and Chapter 5 will provide the networking tools so you can be the better candidate.

What, then, is effective communication? How can you learn to harness these skills in your career so you can have the career of your imagination?

Many books have been written by many experts about communication. You could probably write your own book featuring examples of poor communication you have personally experienced. I have certainly made my fair share of communication blunders. I've wanted to put my foot in my mouth numerous times. I've also observed, studied, and researched what works (and why) and what does not throughout my career.

I have observed that time and time again poor communication skills can prevent an otherwise superb engineer from reaching his or her potential. I have sat in on numerous "state of the industry" panels where senior engineers or business owners bemoan the fact that they can't find qualified engineers that can also carry on a conversation. If you want to be a leader, traits like those discussed in Chapter 2 of being visible, helpful, and building relationships are required. You simply cannot do any of those without solid communication skills.

A 2014 study[30] of engineering employers such as IBM, Chevron, and Seagate Technology found that technical skills did not even make the top five skills desired by employers. While it can be presumed that employers assume if you graduate from a university with an engineering degree you have technical skills, the most valuable skills desired by employers of engineers were (in order of importance):

1. Ability to work in a team

2. Ability to make decisions and solve problems

3. Ability to communicate

In a study by the American Society of Mechanical Engineers, academics were asked if they thought their school provided adequate communication training for engineers. 52 percent of mechanical engineering department heads thought their graduates were strong in this area. In the same study, industry leaders were asked the same question. Industry responded that only 9 percent thought the hired graduates had strong communication skills.[31]

That means 91% of industry (at least in this study) believes engineering communication skills are mediocre at best. With the bar set so low, you don't need to have the speaking skills of a talk-show host or a politician to succeed. With a little practice and focus on basic communication skills, you will be better than most with minimal effort on your part.

But perhaps, like me, being "better than most" is not your goal. You aspire to greatness. You aspire to the upper echelons of your engineering field. If that is the case, focused attention on this subject will put you on an accelerated path to a leadership position not only at your current employer but in your industry. There simply aren't enough engineers that are able to communicate passably, let alone well. There are even fewer engineers who recognize that continuous practice and improvement on their own communication skills is required to have unlimited potential.

In this chapter, you will learn that effective communication starts with mindset. You will learn the most valuable mindset traits (MVT's). You will learn immediate actions to take that will improve your ability to influence others through effective communication.

Emotional Intelligence and the High Performing Team

The Mayfield Handbook of Technical and Scientific Writing states, "Good technical communication is accurate, clear, concise, coherent, and appropriate."[32] Sounds easy—or at least straightforward, right? Here is where your perception and reality conflict.

Skip Weisman studies workplace communication skills for engineers. A recognized expert in this area, he has been quoted in articles for *Forbes* and *U.S. News & World Report.* In a 2015 podcast interview for the Engineering Career Coach (TECC), Weisman tells us that engineers take a sixty-seven percent risk of damaging important relationships with people every time they speak. Why? Trust.[33]

In an interview posted by the Institution of Chemical Engineers (IChemE), Dr. Jamie Cleaver, who holds a doctorate in chemical engineering and whose UK-based company helps technical professionals communicate better, talks about why engineers and scientists struggle to communicate. "[Engineers] are more content looking at systems and equations, looking at how things work, and spending time studying those rather than studying people."[34]

Who purchases engineering products? People. Whose lives may depend on the reliability of our engineering designs? People. But the processes and methods that most engineers are taught often remove people from the equation.

In order to understand precisely how engineers can collectively elevate our communication skills, we must first change our communication mindset to focus on people in addition to processes. How can we communicate in a way that will enable people to understand and respond to our message?

It starts with emotional intelligence, which also happens to be the foundation of high performing teams._People with high emotional intelligence have the ability to pick up on others' emotions. They hear the things that are not being said, and they see the nuances in body language which convey the unspoken. They have the discipline to listen without immediate judgment. They control their own emotions. That discipline, control, and nonjudgmental attitude enable others to feel psychologically safe.

Enabling others to feel safe on a team turns out to be critically important to building a high-performing team, as Google discovered in a study of 180 sales and engineering teams that lasted more than two years.[35] High-performing teams result in more company profits. In a 2013 Deltek study of architecture and engineering firms, Deltek found that profits of high-performing firms are in the range of 25 percent as opposed to an average firm profit of less than 10 percent.[36]

High emotional intelligence is also correlated with individual success. Travis Bradberry, best-selling author of *Emotional Intelligence 2.0*, says in a *Forbes* article:

"Of all the people we've studied at work, we've found that 90% of top performers are also high in emotional intelligence. On the flip side, just 20% of bottom performers are high in emotional intelligence. You can be a top performer without emotional intelligence, but the chances are slim. Naturally, people with a high degree of emotional intelligence make more money—an average of $29,000 more per year than people with a low degree of emotional intelligence.

The link between emotional intelligence and earnings is so direct that every point increase in emotional intelligence was found to add $1,300 to an annual salary. These findings hold true for people in all industries, at all levels, in every region of the world. We haven't yet been able to find a job in which performance and pay aren't tied closely to emotional intelligence."[37]

Most of us have seen a low-performing team in practice. Remember that college "team" project where everyone divided up tasks among themselves and worked individually, and there was always one person who did not complete their work? Or perhaps you've been on a work team where team members walked on eggshells, afraid to share ideas? Or a team where input is sought from everyone, but you know the team leader is going to do what they want, regardless? Did any of these teams inspire your best work? Did you even want to work with any of these teams? This is the very definition of a low-performing team.

So what does a high-performing team do differently? Team members listen to and respect each other, even as ideas are debated. The merits of the idea only (not the person with the idea) are debated, allowing nothing said to be taken personally. High energy is evident. No one person dominates the discussions. The team leader inspires with a clear vision rather than dictating by fear. Team members are trusted to look out for the best interest of the team and each other, and they have a common goal that each member can clearly articulate. They celebrate group successes and they don't point fingers at each other when the inevitable failures occur.

Are you working in a high-performing team? Here's a quick experiment to try in your next meeting or on your next conference call. Write down everyone's initials on a piece of paper and put a check next to a person's name each time they speak. The meetings where a couple people dominate will tend not to be as high-performing as those where everyone speaks. If this happens consistently over time, chances are this team is not high-performing.

What can you do to increase your own emotional intelligence and the performance of every team in which you participate? Remember, turning your team—even if you aren't the team leader—into a high-performing team has been proven to result in higher profits. Do you think you will be rewarded the teams you work with and lead produce more profits?

Honing your emotional intelligence is the key, but how can engineers do this? If you are like me, emotional intelligence sounds like it must be a naturally occurring skill—you were either born with it or not. This could not be further from the truth. Emotional intelligence can be learned and practiced just like you learned your technical expertise. The next section will break down the three things you must learn to unlock your own emotional intelligence. These are the three most valuable communication traits, or MVT's. The MVT's are obnoxious listening, positive thinking, and calm in chaos.

MVT #1: Obnoxious listening

We live in an age where we can post our opinions on social media immediately for the world to see. Controversial posts go viral more quickly than status-quo, resulting in a constant search for tweetable talking points. We receive continuous notifications from Facebook, Instagram, and Twitter (just to name a few) on our devices. Our phones sit on the table when we eat, and they are in our hands when we are socializing at a party.

In physical meetings, we split our attention between the meeting and our email. Our minds wander to what we either did before the meeting or everything we need to get done after. We are constantly on the go, moving from work to home to play and back again. We "hear" many things going on in the world around us, but much of it is noise. "How are you doing today?" we say, greeting busy coworkers, colleagues, and clients, but we really don't want a reply other than "fine" to that question.

We hear but don't listen. While someone else is talking, we tune out and think about what we are going to say next in the conversation. We interrupt others when they speak. If someone tells us a story, instead of focusing on the speaker, we are thinking about a time the same thing happened to us so that we can interject with "me too." This results in leaving most conversations, including business meetings, with everyone involved feeling as if they have not been heard or understood by anyone else. Miscommunication is rampant.

We all know someone who has to give their opinion on every subject and has to have the last word, someone who will go out of their way to correct any detail of the conversation—no matter how trivial—if they perceive the conversation is not 100 percent factually correct. For example, you may say, "I need to mow the grass this weekend," to this person around the water cooler. They will reply, "Well, it is going to rain and everyone knows that you can't mow grass in the rain. I think you had better do that tonight since the weather is nice today."

How do interactions like this makes you feel? How do you feel when someone is glancing at their smart phone every few minutes when you are talking to them? Do you have any interest in having a second interaction with someone who constantly interrupts or corrects you while speaking?

Now imagine an interaction with one of your best friends. How does it feel when he or she listens to you and looks you in the eye while listening? How does it feel when they are fully engaged in the conversation and listening to what you say without interruption, correction, or looking at their phone? Do you notice how much more trustworthy this person feels to you than the first scenario? This is obnoxious listening at work. It is fully listening to the other person and observing not just what they are saying but how they feel. It is being fully present for the person with whom you are communicating.

In her book *Wired for Authenticity*,[16] Henna Inam refers to obnoxious listening as "360-degree listening." She describes the following work scenario to illustrate the difference between "hearing" and "listening" in a work environment:

Colleague (Carlos) to the boss: "So you see, we will need about 70 percent of the group's budget to be able to meet our deadlines for this project. As you know, this is on the CEO's radar."

You at normal listening (thinking to yourself): Yeah, yeah, well, my project is important too … Imagine the audacity to ask for 70 percent of the department's budget! I'd better think quickly about what strategic priority my project is linked to. Maybe I should ask for 50 percent.

You at 360-degree listening: Hmm … Carlos is asking for that big budget, but he doesn't seem so confident. The boss looks as if he's about to lose his cool. Wow, I'm noticing myself get a bit nervous knowing I'm next. I wonder what would be the right way for me to approach this.[16]

What can obnoxious listening do for you? It enables you to gain the trust of your team, and it helps create a high-performing team. You learned earlier that higher profits result from high-performing teams. Participating in or creating a high-performing team at work results in your getting noticed, promoted, and becoming an influencer at an accelerated rate.

Obnoxious listening gives you a full understanding of all the issues at hand, not just your preconceived notions of what is important. It helps you avoid miscommunications. It enables you to pick up on the all-important language of nonverbal communication that will be discussed in the next chapter.

Right now, though, let's put obnoxious listening to work in a meeting. Remember the meeting experiment where you wrote down how often everyone spoke? Let's say you are running the meeting and notice that a team member—let's call him Luke—has not said a word the entire meeting. In this case, you could stop the meeting and say, "Luke, tell me what you think about this." Alternately, if you are simply a participant in the meeting, you can say, "I notice Luke has not told us what he thinks, and I'd really like to hear his opinion."

Active listeners make the people they are speaking with feel as if they are the only person in the room. Celebrities like Bill Clinton and Oprah use this talent to make millions of dollars each year. Studies show that 55 percent of the meaning in communication is conveyed non-verbally, and 38 percent is indicated by the vocal tone, while only 7 percent is conveyed by the speaker's message.[38] Most engineers make the mistake of focusing on the message—which only accounts for 7% of communication—when they should be focusing on improving higher-percentage communication tasks. Many people I have met—including but certainly not limited to engineers—do not know how to listen.

In her blog post "Listen Like Oprah," Jane Adshead-Grant talks about the three most common barriers to listening, which are usually environmental (distractions such as smartphones or being hungry). However, in my experience, the most common communication sin for engineers is not environmental. It is the "rebuttal tendency"— the tendency of our detail-oriented minds to develop a counterargument while the speaker is still speaking. In action, this shows up as "correcting" another while speaking, interrupting someone to interject your (perceived) "correct" approach, or generally expecting all verbal messages to be factually accurate.

One of our strengths as engineers is our precise approach to the world. However, every time we correct, interrupt, or start telling others why they are wrong in conversation, we break our listener's trust and show that while we are receiving the conversational message, we are not really listening. We are not paying attention to the 93% of communication that is not the verbal message. If you are anything like me, you can recall numerous times where you have done this either at work or at home.

There *are* appropriate times to correct others—for example, if someone is doing an engineering analysis incorrectly. But we need to stop thinking about what we will say while others are speaking. We need to stop correcting someone in both our minds and with our voices. Telling Craig that the reason he got stuck in traffic and was late to a meeting was because he did not know the best way to go (according to you) will result in Craig thinking you are judgmental and don't understand him. You have broken Craig's emotional trust in a situation where being right or wrong really didn't matter. That makes him much less likely to contribute his expertise to the meeting because he believes he will be judged.

What should we do instead? We should empathize with Craig, even if we don't agree or are upset that he was late. We can use terms such as "tell me more" and "what else?" when speaking with others. We can restate what we have heard to show we are listening and understand. We can ask questions like "how" or "why" to learn more. Instead of saying to Craig, "If you had traveled this way, you would have been on time," you could say instead, "Craig, you are telling me there was a car accident that caused you to be late. I am so thankful you were not involved and am happy you made it here in one piece. Now, tell me more about [enter technical subject matter at hand]." Which statement encourages Craig to share his creative technical ideas? Which statement hinders Craig's creativity because he fears your judgment before the meeting even starts?

You become an engineering leader by creating trust. Trust allows everyone around you to safely share their best ideas. Through practice, you enhance your capability for emotional intelligence. You learn to mindfully listen and "hear" body language in addition to the spoken word. Obnoxious listening is the foundation of unlocking the key to emotional intelligence so you can accelerate your engineering career. It is the single most important trait you can cultivate as an exceptional engineer.

MVT #2: Positive thinking

Positive thinking is the second-most valuable trait. What is positive thinking? This is not the blindly optimistic person who always looks on the bright side. Rather, it is the person who sees a challenge as an opportunity instead of an obstacle. A positive thinker believes she can have an impact, no matter the situation. She thinks big, instead of small.

Positive thinking inspires positive action in others. Think about the person who recovers from cancer to run a marathon or overcomes great obstacles to succeed. Those people will garner respect regardless of the industry in which they work. They influence with inspiration. You don't have to overcome an obstacle like cancer to use this communication skill—just don't be a negative Nellie. No one wants to be around people who are always negative.

Positive-to-negative interaction ratios significantly impact work productivity and happiness. Scientists have studied the optimum positive-to-negative ratios on work teams and found that an optimum ratio is three positives to one negative. People working on teams with this ratio (or greater) are much more productive than teams with a lower ratio. The scientists found an upper bound of 13:1 (that would be the rose-colored glasses approach), but most organizational teams don't even approach the 3:1 ratio.[39]

How do we demonstrate positive thinking? What does a positive interaction look like at work? Consider this scenario:

Michelle is a star employee. Today, when she walked into the office, the administrative assistant greeted her by name and chatted with her for a few minutes about her activities the evening before (positive 1, negative 0). Then Michelle sat down to read her messages and was confronted with an email from a coworker complaining about a project she is working on (positive 1, negative 1). Michelle responded to the email, and then took a coffee break where a different coworker tells her how impressed they were with a presentation she had given last week (positive 2, negative 1). When Michelle got back to her desk, a client called to thank her for getting him the information he needed so quickly and asks some additional questions (positive 3, negative 1). The call went long, however, resulting in Michelle being late for an internal staffing meeting.

When Michelle arrived at the meeting, she immediately apologized to those in the meeting (even though it was not her fault the call ran long and this was an important client). However, the person running the meeting commented, "Well, now we can get started, albeit five minutes late." The jab hits Michelle since she already apologized. Instead of contributing to the meeting, Michelle sits in the meeting feeling bad for being late (positive 3, negative 2).

What happens when our positive-to-negative ratio drops below 3:1 at work? Over time, the same study showed this results in employee disengagement. Low engagement results in low-performing teams. Low-performing teams results in lower profits.

But that is not who YOU are. You are a high performer and aspire to be one of the best in your field. That means you purposefully create and seek out positive interactions. As our example with Michelle shows, having a naturally cheerful, bubbly personality has nothing to do with creating positive interactions. It has everything to do with cultivating a positive mindset.

Psychological research shows that once we "make up our mind" about something, we usually don't change it. If we associate going to the dentist with getting a root canal, that association will make us dread going to the dentist. If we have decided someone is a jerk at work, we will always view our interactions with that person through the lens of them being a "jerk," looking for real or imagined slights. We look for "proof" to back up our preconceived notions. The psychological term for this natural tendency is "confirmation bias."

Studies on confirmation bias show that if I show jerk-like behavior, I attribute it to an external factor, such as being tired or hungry. If *you* are a jerk, however, my brain decides it is a character flaw. This will affect all my interactions with you and potentially cause me to be unable to be positive with you unless I am aware and mindful of my preconceptions.

In Chapter 1 we talked about how each of us has the ability to choose to be happy in life and in work. We can choose to believe that we create our own circumstances, which is the very definition of thinking positively.

When we choose to see ourselves as a driver of our lives rather than a victim, others will flock to our positive energy. We become a leader in words, thoughts, and deeds. We become an influencer that others want to follow. In becoming a leader, we put ourselves in position for the best projects and desired promotions, and we become the best engineer (and person) we can possibly become.

Make up your mind today to be happy in life and in work. You deserve no less. Feeling down or frustrated with your current situation? Take action (or at least make a plan) to correct it. In the meantime, write a gratitude journal or a thank-you letter to someone who has inspired you, or simply start increasing your interactions with other positive people.

Engineers tend to be phenomenally organized and detail-oriented. However, the same traits that make us great engineers often cause us to fail to live in the moment. That high-achieving drive can result in feeling that we are never good enough. Negative thoughts lead to negative attitudes. Negative attitudes hold us back from reaching our full potential. Negative attitudes cause us to think small when we should be thinking big.

Cultivate a positive attitude by expressing gratitude daily. For example, you could start by thinking of three very specific things for which you are thankful; this can be as basic as a beautiful sunrise. Over time, gratitude becomes an ingrained habit. Do you want to work with or for someone who is thankful and appreciative of your talents or someone who interacts primarily with their colleagues when something goes wrong or they need something? Display the behavior in yourself that you want to see in others.

When you encounter the jerks or negative people at work, you have two options. If the work culture is consistently negative, I strongly recommend looking for a new work team or position because the negative energy will drag you down over time and lead to disengagement, no matter your natural optimism levels. Not sure if you are in a negative environment? Gain some hard data by keeping track of your negative-to-positive ratios for a day or a week like we did with Michelle.

If there is one person in your life that is particularly negative, limit your interactions with that person. If they are at work, don't talk to them extensively at the water cooler or socially. Instead, limit your interactions to business only. If this person is a coworker (and not your manager or boss), this can be very effective. Once again, however, if this *is* your manager or boss, you will want to find a new job or volunteer for another team as quickly as possible. Otherwise, you will eventually be sucked into their negative energy.

MVT #3: Calm in chaos

The third-most valuable trait is the ability to remain calm in chaos. 90 percent of top performers displayed this trait in a study of over one million people.[40] It's easy to be calm when everything is going well, but most people agree that the way someone performs when things are not going well is the measure of that person's character. If you are like me, this may be the most challenging of the MVT's to practice. It's one I struggle with the most, but is also the one where I notice immediate benefits when I successfully apply it.

To understand how to remain calm, we first have to understand what happens to our bodies when under stress. What happens to your body when you make a mistake, you have a fight with a friend, or you are behind on an impending deadline? Your "fight-or-flight" biochemical reaction kicks in as the emotions evoked by memories stored in the brain's amygdala alert you to a stressful situation, which sends that emotional memory message from the brain to your adrenal glands. The adrenal glands, in turn, release hormones in preparation for immediate physical action. The hormones cause your breathing and heart rates in increase. You may feel panic or fear. By preparing your body for a physical reaction instead of a thinking reaction, the hormones hijack the logical part of your brain. Your capacities for thinking, reasoning, and making logical decisions are diminished until the hormones disappear.

This means it is very important to stay calm in the event of a crisis if you need to make decisions. Because leaders are required to make effective decisions in chaotic situations, this leadership trait—especially when used in combination with the previous MVTs—will set you apart. The good news is that you can train yourself to avoid allowing your emotional state to hijack your brain.

In their book *Leading from the Front*,[41] US Marines Angie Morgan and Courtney Lynch discuss how emotional outbursts—even crying one time at work—can destroy your credibility regardless of gender. Courtney tells the story of a young (male) corporal who became emotional one day when being reprimanded for failure to obey orders as a young Marine. "Tears change the relationship between you and your colleagues or teammates," she writes. "Crying in front of others creates an uncomfortable situation and interferes with your ability to lead. Work on controlling your emotions so that your reputation as a leader isn't damaged."

Routinely crying at work will make it very difficult to get valid feedback. No one wants to hurt your feelings enough to make you cry. However, as engineers both positive and negative feedback is required for you to grow. If your manager is concerned that feedback will result in an emotional outburst, it is likely you won't get ANY feedback at all. That means you won't know where your blind spots are or what you need to work on to grow. Engineers that can't be trusted to control their emotions at work are unlikely to be assigned the most interesting or high-profile projects necessary to become a high performer.

Women walk a tightrope here that men don't need to walk. Because our competence is linked with our likeability, taking too much emotion out of the equation can mean we present as "cold" or "unfeeling" in the face of crisis. Expressing strong emotions—and notice I said "expressing," which is entirely different from "feeling" that emotion—is a career killer for both sexes that will limit your leadership potential. This includes crying at work, yelling (although in some fields men can get away with this), knee-jerk reactions, and being overly sensitive to criticism.

It's hard to learn to not take things personally at times, especially when you are passionate about your work and the quality of your work product. It's hard to not take offense when you have been working overtime for weeks on a project, only to have a client declare he does not like the concept and you have to start over. It's hard when a manager asks you to pile one more project onto your already overloaded schedule. It's hard when someone on your own team starts pointing figures at you or other individuals on the team. These things or similar have happened to me and will happen to you at some point in your engineering career. Fortunately for us, remaining calm can be learned.

Remember, in order to make a good decision, you need to clearly understand the situation. Expressing emotions in an unhealthy way—such as crying, yelling, or assigning blame—is a waste of energy that could be used to better understand and solve the problem. Focusing on solutions first helps you detach from the situation, which avoids the secretion of those annoying brain-hijacking hormones.

The reality of being human is that you are going to experience emotions. Try these four methods to quickly move your brain from emotional hijack to logical thought. If you are like me, continual practice over time will dramatically improve your ability to stay calm in the face of crisis.

1. Notice the "freak out" feeling and name it. Think to yourself, "Alert! Brain hijack on the way." Notice how your body is feeling. Are you getting tense? Is your heart racing? Being self-aware of your emotions is the first step to remaining calm. This is because the part of your brain that notices things is the same part that thinks logically. Bonus tip:

learning to be more mindful on a daily basis (see chapter 1) can help cultivate this awareness before you need it.

2. If you feel your emotions welling up, excuse yourself from the situation immediately for a few moments to regain composure. For example, you can take a bathroom break. You can excuse yourself to respond to an emergency email or text. You can pause and walk over to the water cooler in a large meeting room to get a drink. Your goal is to "pause" the situation to give yourself the opportunity to take a few deep breaths and regroup.

3. Distance yourself emotionally from the situation to gain perspective. Ask and answer the following questions in your head:

   a. Is this problem important enough that you will remember it next year at this time?

   b. If today was your last day on earth, would you still feel this way about this situation? Or is this chaos simply drama that does not really matter?

   c. If a friend came to you for advice on this crisis, what would you tell them?

4. If you are not in the heat of the moment, make sure you have a physical outlet for stress. Stress build-up eventually requires release, either in the form of exercise or an unhealthy emotional response. Researchers at Princeton University found that exercise over time causes a fundamental change to brain chemistry. Exercise causes more stress-inhibiting hormones to occupy the active brain as compared to the sedentary brain.[42] Remember how we talked about taking care of yourself in Chapter 1? We reap the benefits in our ability to stay calm here.

Chapter 3 – What you learned

In this chapter you discovered why engineers must learn and demonstrate communication skills to become leaders in their technical areas. You learned that enhanced communication skills results in trust. Trust is required for high-performing teams. High-performing teams result in measurably greater profits. You learned that in order to create trust you must hone your emotional intelligence through the MVT's of obnoxious listening, positive thinking, and remaining calm in chaos. You practiced methods of applying these traits so you can become an influencer in your field.

In the next chapter, you will learn how to use the emotional intelligence you developed in this chapter and apply it to communication tasks specific to your engineering work, such as technical writing and speaking. You have valuable knowledge to share, and the next chapter will give you the tools to make sure your message is heard and acted upon. You will leave Chapter 4 with a how-to toolkit to instantly build the trust of those around you and become the leading engineer you are meant to be.

Chapter 3—Career acceleration challenge

1. Listen: For 30 minutes at your next social event, don't interrupt or correct anyone when speaking. Instead, when there is a pause in the conversation, say, "tell me more" or "what else?" Notice how the person you are talking to responds.

2. Positive Thinking: Complete a 30 minute "no-complaining" challenge. Do not complain about anything, even in your head. This includes any negative self-talk. For example: I look terrible in this outfit, I can't figure out how to do this, etc. If you do complain, you must start the challenge over again until you successfully complete all 30 minutes. Bonus challenge and prep for the Chapter 4 challenges: Can you do this for one full day?

3. Calmness: Promote calmness in your life. Download a free mediation app (Calm or Headspace are two popular ones at the time of book publication). Try it for 10 minutes a day.

Chapter 4

ENGINEERING
COMMUNICATION
IN ACTION

In Chapter 3, you learned how to speak the communication language of leaders. You discovered the importance of tuning into your emotional intelligence capabilities to create a high-performing team. You learned how to create trust—the crucial component for a high-performing team—through the three MVT's of obnoxious listening, positive thinking, and remaining calm in chaos. You learned that practicing these skills will accelerate your path to the top of your field when combined with your technical expertise.

Eighty percent of our waking hours are spent in communication. How are these hours spent? The typical person spends 25 percent of communication time writing, 30 percent speaking, and 45 percent listening. Chapter 4 will teach you specific applications for engineers in each of these three areas. You'll learn best practices and practical tips for real-life situations you will encounter in your career. This chapter will show you how to apply the specific communication types—written, verbal, and nonverbal—in an engineering context so your message is received clearly and accurately.

Chapter 4 will teach you how to find your voice and become a confident speaker. You will learn tools and tips to successfully communicate with bosses, coworkers, and clients, and how to avoid common communication pitfalls unique to women. You will learn the *one* rule of effective communication. You will leave this chapter with techniques to craft a message that resonates with your audience so you can become an influencer in your field.

Communication types at work: written, verbal and nonverbal

Written communication

Sixteen-year-old Maryland resident Amber Marie Rose died when she crashed her car into a tree. The cause of the crash? The faulty ignition switch in her 2005 Chevrolet Cobalt had turned off the car's electrical system and additionally caused her airbag deployment to fail.[43] In 2015, General Motors, the manufacturer of the Cobalt, reached a settlement over the 124 fatalities and the 274 injuries found to be caused by this same defect.[44] Reviewing the 315-page internal GM investigation report, *Forbes* contributor Carmine Gallo observed that many of these deaths could have been prevented if proper communication was used in the initial reports:

"Group after group and committee after committee within GM that reviewed the issue failed to take action or acted too slowly." The report shows that they acted slowly due to improper word choice. From the beginning the problem with the ignition switch had been labeled as a "customer convenience" issue. Those two words left people with the impression that the problem simply annoyed some drivers instead of giving GM experts and managers the more accurate assessment that the problem was a major safety defect that could potentially kill people.[45]

Clearly the GM story is much more complex than a communication breakdown. But what if those two words in the report had been revised to say "life safety" instead of "customer convenience"? How many lives may have been saved and injuries prevented? Engineers and scientists—perhaps more so than any other profession—must carefully consider their audience and communicate in such a way that the risks can be understood by nontechnical readers. We have no way of knowing if that was the engineers' original wording of the report. All we know is that the engineers' working knowledge of the problem was not communicated effectively to those who needed to mobilize the solution (who typically have a nontechnical background).

Technical report writing will be required of almost every engineer at some point in their career. In the offices in which I have worked, writing is often seen as a necessary evil that is not considered "real" engineering work, especially by engineers who have recently graduated from college. This is a myth.

For most engineers, the technical writing "training" you may have received was a single course in college that may or may not relate to translating complex analysis into material understandable by less technical readers. For working engineers, it's unlikely you have received any writing training since that single college course. But as we look at the destruction of lives poor technical writing can cause, you begin to see some of the reasons that make developing this skill set so important.

If you are like me, you may not have the time or interest to enhance your technical writing skills beyond your formal education. That's why I've compiled six tips for technical writing that will immediately improve your ability to craft a message that resonates with your audience if applied.

1. Know your audience – Who is the target of your written word? Provide the written information they need from the reader's point of view, not yours. You MUST use different language to write a technical user manual for a peer engineer in your office than you would if you are writing a publicly posted blog.

2. Be concise and specific – Avoid run-on sentences and get to the point. Consider whether your audience (see #1) will understand the background information behind your points. If not, simplify the message. Let's say you are charged with investigating a new software program that your company may purchase. Instead of saying (vaguely), "This new software will potentially help us save money and increase productivity," say, "This software will save us money. The initial price point is 10 percent less. We tested a free trial version and found it reduced analysis time in our trial problems by 5 percent."

3. Avoid technical jargon, particularly if you are not writing for a technical crowd – The point of writing is not to show how smart you are. The point is to share your information with the audience. The one exception here is writing for a technical journal where your audience is only peer engineers.

4. Keep to the facts – Emotions do not belong in technical writing. Avoid using terms such as "I feel," "I believe," and "I hope" in writing. Technical writing—including and especially email—is not the place for angry words or venting frustration. We can evoke emotion through stories and facts without stating our personal emotions. And that angry email? Go ahead and write it—but wait until the next day to decide what to do with it. If you would not want that angry email accidentally forwarded to your mother, it's best to rephrase prior to sending or delete it.

5. The "we's" have it – Your audience doesn't care about you; they care about what you can do for them. Either replace all your "I's" with "we's" or write from a third-party voice (especially for technical manuals). The email that says, "I think your engineering analysis is wrong," sounds very different from, "We are finding some discrepancies in your technical analysis. Tell us more about your approach to this problem."

6. Active voice – Our messages are more concise when we use active voice instead of passive voice. Instead of saying, "Professional engineering licensure was found to be necessary specific to structural engineering in only ten states," say, "Only ten states require professional structural engineering licensure."

Verbal communication: finding your voice

Skilled orators capture a room when speaking. They hold an audience captive to their words and can seemingly talk anyone into almost anything. They have enormous influence in the world. Martin Luther

King Jr. inspired a generation of civil rights activists with his "I have a dream" speech. Hitler incited a war with his speaking skills. Oprah, Barack Obama, Winston Churchill, and Steve Jobs can all attribute much of their success and influence to their speaking skills. If we aspire to be an influential engineer, we can learn a lot from the speaking skills of great orators. And guess what? They didn't start out as great speakers. They *learned* how to be great speakers.

Fortunately for us, engineers usually don't have to become great orators—we simply need to be able to have a conversation. "Being able to hold a meaningful dialogue with a friend, colleague, boss, or potential business partner is an invaluable talent and one which most people don't spend much time cultivating," says public radio broadcaster Celeste Headlee, in her wildly popular TED Talk.

In the age of electronic communication, the ability to have a conversation is on the fast track to extinction. We'd rather text on our phones than talk to a live person. At the same time, engineers who can hold a conversation and are not afraid of public speaking are in higher demand than ever. This section will show you how to find and use your voice to create more influence at work.

Finding your voice: voice and pitch

In her book *Executive Presence*[46], Sylvia Hewlett discusses the common flaws in speaking skills that were cited by business executives in her study. The obvious culprits were things like being inarticulate, using poor grammar, having a strong accent, or using filler words, such as "uh," "you know," and "like." The less obvious, however, were timbre and pitch of the voice. Sylvia writes:

"Everybody seemed to recall an annoying voice, one that was too high-pitched, or too mousy, too breathy or too raspy. In particular, those we interviewed mentioned "shrill" women: women who, whenever they get emotional or defensive, raise the timbre of their voice, turning off coworkers and clients, and losing out on leadership opportunities."

There is a limited timbre and pitch range in which most people are comfortable hearing speaking voices. The range for those that exude "leadership presence" is even less. A large percentage of men's voices tend to fall into that range, while the majority of women's voices will fall out of this range, especially in the higher registers. Numerous studies have shown that deeper voices are associated with leadership positions.[46]

In a study of male CEOs, a 1 percent decrease in voice pitch was linked to a $30 million increase in the size of his company. This in turn lead to greater compensation for CEO's with larger companies. The average CEO in the study comes in at 125.5 Hz, which is about average for an adult male.[47] In comparison, an average female voice is in the range of 200–230 Hz. It should be noted that this particular study did not include female CEOs.

You may be wondering how voices in these ranges sound. James Earl Jones, the voice of Darth Vader, has a voice pitched at around 85 Hz, Julia Roberts is around 171 Hz, and Roseanne Barr, who most of us can agree has a voice in the "shrill" category, is pitched around 377 Hz.[48]

We also know that most of us change our voice pitch depending on the situation. If you are in a room with someone talking on the phone, can you tell their relationship with the person on the other end of the line? It is likely you can simply by the pitch of their voice. Men and women talk to children and loved ones in higher-pitched voices. They lower their voices when in a serious meeting or situation. Culturally we have associated those lower pitches with leadership. Is that view technically sexist? Probably, but most won't see it that way. More importantly, not one engineering manager I've ever run into would dare give you feedback that your voice is too high-pitched for you to advance in the company.[49]

Female engineers need to be aware of this scientific vocal phenomenon. Once aware, most women will start modulating their voices into the most natural lower register available until it becomes second nature. Margaret Thatcher did this with the help of a voice coach after BBC famously dropped her from a political spot because her voice was too harsh. She then went on to become Great Britain's prime minister from 1979-1990.

Finding your voice: craft a clear message

Most of us were taught to "think before you speak" when we were children. Thinking enables us to craft a clear message in our heads before we share our thoughts with the world. It's well known that men tend to speak less in general than women, so in the engineering world, women need to be especially aware of our natural tendency to "think aloud" and discuss all options available—usually out loud—before making a decision.

That natural tendency we have to "think aloud" can come across as being unsure of ourselves or indecisive in some situations. Speaking concisely and getting to the point projects confidence for both genders. Remember that how you say something is more important than what you say, particularly if you are supplying information to someone who needs to make a decision. The hippocampus is the part of our brain that makes decisions, and it does not respond to verbal cues. However, the hippocampus does respond to feelings, and scientific studies have proven that speaking in a confident manner is important regardless of the message.

Women are more likely than men to use a number of speaking practices that undermine our messages, many of which involve using filler words such as "sorry" or "just" to couch a demand as a request. The use of passive-aggressive language or overly qualifying statements also results in the same outcome: a message that is unclear to the receiver. You may say to your supervisor in your first project, "I just want to say that I believe my analysis is complete, but I'm not sure if I used the correct assumptions." Consider how that sounds and then imagine saying instead, "My analysis is correct assuming my assumptions are valid. Can you review these with me?" If YOU were the supervisor, which statement would inspire confidence in your work?

I am constantly amazed by how often women (myself included) apologize when speaking. "I'm sorry for your bad day," you may say to a friend (as if the bad day was your fault). "Sorry," you may say after someone bumps into you on the sidewalk.

Why do women do this? Studies show that while women and men both apologize, women have a lower threshold for behavior that is offensive.[50] "Habitually over-apologizing—saying 'sorry' when you mean 'excuse me,' or just to ease tension when you've done nothing wrong—can work against you," explains Bryan Dik, PhD, associate professor of psychology at Colorado State University and cofounder of jobzology.com. "Chronically apologizing for things that aren't your fault can hurt your self-esteem, make other people uncomfortable, and let the offender off the hook."[51]

Over-apologizing also signals to others a lack of confidence. If you take nothing else from this section, delete "sorry" from all emails forevermore, unless you truly are fully responsible.

Other examples of speaking "don'ts" are up-speak (the practice of ending what should be a statement with a question mark), complaining, and gossiping. When was the last time you were inspired into positive action by someone's negative comments? Likely never.

Leaders don't complain; they problem solve. Negative people say, "This is a problem." Following that statement, they grumble about precisely what is wrong, assigning blame to whomever they perceive is at fault. Leaders say, "What about this is good, and how can we improve it?" Which person would you prefer to work with? Which one are you more likely to respect or assist if they ask for help? Which person is ultimately much more likely to be promoted or work on critical projects?

We all have bad days, and it's OK to vent to your journal and occasionally to your friends. But we need to be aware that our negative thoughts, words, and actions drag ourselves and others around us down. That is a waste of energy and time for anyone who wants to excel in life.

Finding your voice: presenting and speaking formally

"According to most studies, people's number one fear is public speaking. Number two is death. Death is number two. Does that seem right? That means to the average person, if you have to go to a funeral, you're better off in the casket than doing the eulogy." *Jerry Seinfeld*[62]

Clammy hands, fast breathing, shaking, and heart racing with fear … does this sound familiar? No, I was not running a marathon. I was getting ready to give my first speech (written on the paper in front of me, not memorized) in front of a group of peers and parents in my elementary school. Fast-forward twenty years, and I am about to give a presentation to a group of engineering peers at a national conference. Clammy hands? Check. Increased heart rate? Check. Shaking? A little. Heart racing with fear? Nope. Now it's racing with excitement. I get to share my expertise with the world, and I never know what the audience will teach me.

If you are a naturally gifted speaker, you may want to skip ahead to the next chapter, but if you are not, I am here to help you learn because I can't emphasize this enough: if you want to excel as an engineer, it is imperative that you are able to speak in public. That includes developing the ability to give a presentation in front of your boss, peers, and clients.

That is not to say that you need to be an *expert* public speaker. There is no need to be as comfortable presenting as you are tinkering with the inner workings of your computer. Instead, your goal is to be able to confidently express yourself out loud, which includes speaking up at work, in a meeting, or when presenting. It means volunteering for presenting opportunities where you can find them because if you can speak competently, you will stand out positively. If you are proactive enough to excel in this, you will propel yourself to a high level quickly. There is an enormous need for people who can bridge the technical/nontechnical gap.

Learning to be a competent speaker is a process like any other. There's no magic to it. All you need to do is actively practice, get feedback, and practice more. Do you think politicians stand up and deliver the perfect speech the first time? No. They have spent hours practicing and rewriting the speech with a team of experts around them.

Below are four practical ways to practice verbal communication and presenting in a low-risk environment.

1. Join Toastmasters, an organization that will help you get over the fear of speaking in front of strangers. Most towns have at least one group (mine has three). For more information, go to www.toastmasters.org

2. Give an engineering presentation to kids. This does a few things. First, none of those kids will know if anything you say is not precisely accurate, which puts most of the pressure on your presentation style and ability to engage your audience. This is often an area where most speakers, including engineers, need work. It is more difficult to keep the attention of elementary-age children than engineering peers. The kids don't care how smart you are. They only care that you can entertain, making them an excellent group on which to practice. You do not need to make this "presentation" to a formal class. Grab your own kids, or some nieces and nephews if needed.

3. Use volunteer opportunities to hone your presentation skills. Pick a volunteer group you are passionate about and look for ways to hone your skills. For example, if you already volunteer for Habit for Humanity but are petrified of public speaking, offer to give the introduction at the next event or lunch meeting.

4. Give a lunch-and-learn at your office about a topic on which you are the office "expert." You don't need to be a world-famous expert, but I guarantee there is something you know more about than anyone else in your office. You may have attended a conference or recently researched a new technology you can share with the group. Once again, this does not have to be an extensive or formal presentation. Simply write down what you want to share, practice a few

times in advance, and share what you know. You will find that practicing out loud—rather than composing on the fly—enables you to arrive at a clear, concise message.

Nonverbal communication

Nonverbal communication is a critical component of becoming emotionally intelligent. As we discussed in chapter 3, emotional intelligence is required for high-performing teams—and associated higher profits—to exist. By extension, mastering nonverbal communication alone will distinguish you as leadership material. Nonverbal communication in two areas must be developed: your ability to read others' nonverbal communication and aligning your verbal messages with your nonverbal signals.

Everyone has experience in nonverbal communication. For engineers, our detail-oriented minds simply need to become more attuned to the conversation not being spoken. You already have some experience in reading nonverbal communication. Prove it to yourself with this experiment: Turn on a movie. Hit the mute button on the remote. Watch for a few minutes. Can you tell what the person is saying by looking at them? If so, you are successfully reading their body language.

Carol Goman, author of *The Silent Language of Leaders: How Body Language Can Help—or Hurt—How You Lead*, discusses how two people can send more than 800 nonverbal signals in a thirty-minute negotiation. In a *Forbes* article, she writes:

"When your words and your body language are out of alignment, you don't make sense. Neuroscientists use electroencephalograph (EEG) machines to measure "event related potentials"—brain waves that form peaks and valleys. One of these valleys, dubbed N400, occurs when people are shown gestures that contradict what's spoken. This is the same brain wave dip that happens when listening to nonsensical language."[53]

Body language must therefore align with verbal communication. If not, your verbal message is confusing and inauthentic to the person receiving the message. Think about the person who says, "Nice to meet you," but does not shake your hand, or someone who says they are open to feedback while using "closed" body language, such as crossing their arms or legs. Their verbal message is saying one thing and their body language the opposite.

You must learn to understand the cues given and received through body language. Four very specific ways you can start using body language immediately to increase your effectiveness at work are as follows.

1. Take up space, both physically and with stuff. The larger your physical footprint, the more influence and confidence you are perceived to have. Chapter 5 will teach you more about why this works.

2. Sit or stand tall with your shoulders back and head held high. Your mom was right when she said not to slouch.

3. Use eye contact. Looking others in the eye when communicating signals confidence.

4. Adopt powerful body language at appropriate times. Why? Because expansive body language makes us feel more confident. Amy Cuddy, author of the book *Presence*, gives us some examples, such as the "Wonder Woman" pose. Try it by putting your hands on your hips and standing tall with your head back and feet set shoulder-width apart.[54]

Use body language while speaking to demonstrate confidence and authority. While not universal across cultures, in the United States men are much more likely to have adopted expansive postures. Women are usually socially conditioned to use more submissive body language. That means that, as a confident woman, you are much more likely to demonstrate a potential conflict between your message and your body language simply because you have been unconsciously conditioned from birth to use submissive postures. These are easy to correct once you are aware of them. Stop sabotaging your own message by putting an immediate stop to the following three behaviors:

1. Do not touch your hair or face. This includes tucking your hair behind your ear and twirling or combing your hair, etc. unless you are in a bathroom. This also includes leaning your chin on your hand. These behaviors indicate nervousness and lack of confidence to those watching, and many women are not aware that they do this. If this is a habit of yours, consider wearing your hair up when at the office for a period of time to break the habit. Hairstyles such as a simple bun or French twist are easy (especially with second-day hair) and look professional.

2. Stop crossing your legs or arms. This indicates to others that you are either disengaged or combative. The challenge with this one for women is that we often do this when we are cold—and meeting rooms are always freezing! As someone who is usually cold (especially in air conditioning), I have started wearing a blazer or jacket most of the time. This seems to both stop the cold and lend an extra layer of professionalism.

3. Avoiding eye contact can make you appear unsure of yourself at best, or dishonest at worst. Don't stare. Instead, let the person talking to you break eye contact first.

How do you know if your body language is impacting your effectiveness at work, particularly in a negative way? Most managers and bosses in firms with engineers will have difficulty giving direct feedback on body language, but they may be able to give you feedback on your "presence" and "command of the room." Negative feedback in these areas indicates your body language is at least partially to blame.

When you know you need to work on it, the best way to improve your body language is to record yourself speaking or giving a presentation and play it back. I like to do this when I practice the presentation. Similar to the movie experiment, mute yourself and watch your nonverbal cues. Do they project confidence and competence? Nervousness? Do you touch your hair or fidget? Are you relaxed or standing rigidly?

Practice speaking until your nonverbal cues match your confidence in your knowledge. If you want to see some great examples of good body language, google "TED Talks." They are 20 minutes or less each and can give you some great insights into how professional body language appears.

Putting written, verbal, and nonverbal communication together: how to communicate at work

Now that you have learned the three components of engineering communication, it is time to learn how these apply practically at work. How should you be communicating at work in order to maximize your influence?

Interactions that enable you to both hear verbal communication and see body language will always be the most valuable interactions in terms of the amount of information that can be gleamed. Seeing the person with whom you are speaking both enables you to read between the lines and ask better questions in a way that other communication methods cannot.

Business organizations use a hodgepodge of communication styles in the workplace. Different generations often prefer different styles of communication. For example, in my experience, older engineers tend to value face-to-face interactions, while those under thirty prefer texting. Email misuse is abundantly rampant in most age groups. I know a couple of engineers that are known for writing thesis-length emails. Others use emails to avoid confrontation when a face-to-face discussion or phone call would be much more appropriate. Some seem to believe "reply all" should be used for every email.

With this in mind, let's look at how engineers should be communicating in the modern workplace if the goal is to get our message across in the most efficient way possible. Since body language provides more information than words, it is not a surprise that the most effective forms of work communications involve visual interaction. If effective communication is defined as getting your message across quickly and leaving little room for others to interpret your message differently than you intended, the following list—in order of effectiveness—should be used.

1. Verbal in-person communication is the best interaction type because it offers a richness of both verbal and nonverbal communication, which means there is the least chance for misinterpretations and/or misunderstandings of the information being shared. It allows for the use of emotional intelligence to ask questions based on nonverbal cues, which will result in better information sharing. This type of communication should always be your first choice if you need to have either a difficult or a complicated conversation. Examples can include delivering bad news or asking for a raise.

2. Video conferences allow you to see the people with whom you are communicating. This is more effective than other forms of virtual communication and can be very close in effectiveness to No. 1 (verbal in-person communication). However, its effectiveness can be diminished by video quality and lighting of the room or computer. Nuances of body language can be lost in some cases as well.

3. Phone calls should be your first choice of communication if No. 1 and No. 2 are not available and an item requires discussion.

4. Email is most appropriate when summarizing conversations or short answers. However, for many of us, it has become our default method of communication. The average person receives eighty-eight emails per day[55], and researchers have found that constantly responding to emails has tanked our productivity levels. A study of 1,000 white-collar workers

showed that they checked email for 4.1 hours per day each day during the work week. How much real work can you get done if you are constantly checking email?

Email should never be used for difficult conversations because it is simply too easy to misinterpret. We have all received emails that we spent hours second-guessing: "What did she mean by that?" Email should also not be used for a long conversation. If you've sent two emails about one subject and a question is not resolved, you need to elevate the communication level to the No. 1, No. 2, and/or No. 3 methods. Otherwise, you are simply wasting time.

5. Texting or chatting is great for friends, family, and coworkers (many companies have set up an informal chat to facilitate cross-company communication). However, texts should generally be avoided for both groups and external business communication. Unless your client has expressed a preference for text messages, never send your client a text. Similar to email, it is easy to misinterpret if it is anything but a transactional comment.

The one cardinal rule of effectively communicating at work is to follow the platinum rule: Communicate with others as they want you to communicate with them, not in the way you want to communicate. If you are not sure how they would like to be communicate, ASK! If your client prefers a phone call but you prefer email, call them and follow up with an email. An older colleague may prefer a phone call while an engineer fresh out of college may want a text. It is your responsibility to change how you communicate to meet your audience's needs if you want your message to be heard.

Chapter 4 – What you learned

In this chapter, you learned the importance of crafting a message that resonates with your audience. You learned that using precise wording in technical writing can save lives. You learned that how you say something has a greater impact on your audience than the message itself. You discovered that communication skills are directly correlated to perceived leadership potential and leadership presence. You learned how you can develop executive presence by practicing the tools learned in this chapter.

This chapter taught you how to use your written, verbal, and nonverbal communication skills at work. You learned the platinum rule of communication. Chapter 5 builds upon the principles learned in the first four chapters. You will learn how to use knowing yourself, technical expertise, and communication skills to become an influencer at meetings and during networking events. Hate networking? Then read on for tools in the next chapter so you can go from quiet to confident at work networking events.

Chapter 4—Career acceleration challenge

You covered a lot of ground in this chapter. So much so, that there are two sets of career acceleration challenges. The "no" list are things you need to eliminate from your communication habits so you can be perceived as a confident woman who knows her stuff. The "yes" list are challenges intended to expand your skills so you can practice influencing others.

Career Acceleration Challenge: No

1. Apologies: Stop unnecessary apologies. Track the number of times you say "sorry" in one day. Unless something is truly your fault, stop using that word. Challenge yourself to replace "sorry" with "excuse me" or simply eliminate the word altogether.

   BONUS tip: Ask a coworker to help keep you accountable. You have to deposit $1 into a charity fund of the coworker's choice every time you apologize unnecessarily.

2. Delete the weak: Replace weak or qualifying words with strong words in both written and verbal contexts. Eliminate the words "like," "just," and "I believe."

3. No "I" in team: Eliminate "I" from all forms of work communication and replace "I" with "we." Start doing this for all emails and verbal communication today.

Career Acceleration Challenge: Yes

1. Positive Vibes: Remember the 30 minute no-complaining challenge in Chapter 3? Do it again, this time for an entire day. The people around you will respond to your positive energy. I guarantee your can-do attitude will start to be noticed.

2. Power Presentation: Step out of your comfort zone and create a 5 minute presentation about your work goals for the year. Ask your boss for a 15 minute meeting to show it to him or her and get feedback.

3. Productivity: Set one day this week where email is only checked and responded to three times during the workday. Observe how you feel when many more tasks than usual are completed. If your boss expects instantaneous email responses, make sure you let him or her know about the one day experiment and report your productivity results to him or her at the end of the day. You will be surprised at how many more tasks you are able to complete!

Chapter 5

MEETINGS AND NETWORKING

In this chapter, you will learn how to expand your influence in meetings and when networking. You will learn how to present yourself as a female engineer in a client-facing role. Because these events trigger imposter feelings for many women in male-dominated industries, we will take a deep dive into specific methods to shut down your inner critic in situations where you may be the only woman in the room.

You will learn what to wear in an engineering office environment—not because female engineers are vain, but because it is often a challenge to figure that out when surrounded by a sea of khakis and you hate pants.

You will learn how to make networking work for you, even if you are an introvert like me. You will learn how to efficiently apply the giving principles discussed in Chapter 1 when networking. You will leave this chapter with the ability to confidently expand your influence so you can open the doors to infinite career possibilities.

Rock your next meeting

Ted is a project manager about to lead his first client meeting. He walks into the room with a smile on his face, greets the client, shakes his hand, and asks about the client's kids. They talk about the local hockey team making the playoffs. After a few minutes of small talk, he sits down to start the meeting, the tone of which is informal and relaxed. In addition to satisfying his engineering concerns, the client leaves the meeting feeling fully engaged in the project. The client feels that his needs have been heard and incorporated into the design.

Sally is also a project manager about to lead her first client meeting; she has spent weeks preparing and knows her subject well. The following day in the same conference room, she walks into the meeting with her mind on the subject matter at hand. Determined to get down to business as quickly as possible and prove her expertise, she moves to the front of the room and avoids all small talk and greetings since they are unrelated to subject of the meeting. She pulls out her laptop and sits at the front with her arms crossed because the room is cold. When the meeting starts, the tone of the meeting is formal, stilted, and transactional. The client leaves thinking that Sally is really smart, but she does not understand him or his needs.

If you are a client, which meeting was more engaging? Which meeting left you with a more positive assessment of Ted and Sally's employer? If you are Ted or Sally's manager and have observed both meetings, are you more likely to assign Ted or Sally to the next project with a new or larger client?

Some women act like Sally because they feel the need to prove themselves. I walked into meetings as a participant early in my career—often as the only female engineer in the room—with a list of points I wanted to make. I spent most of those meetings focusing on what I was going to say when the opportunity presented itself, which limited my ability to be effective. As we learned in Chapter 3, we can't apply obnoxious listening skills if we are thinking about what to say next. We can't activate our emotional intelligence if we are stuck in our own heads.

Other women behave as Sally because they have a confidence crisis, particularly in public speaking situations. This was also a challenge for me early in my career. I felt a vague sense of discomfort in a meeting room full of men, and it did not help that my meetings typically involved men with at least ten years more experience than myself. In a number of cases, I flat-out thought, "I do not belong in this room." I still have to fight this at times, even if I am the one running the meeting. That pesky imposter syndrome has hijacked my mind again!

How can you evict these and similar doubts from your mind? If you are like me, it helps to remember that you were asked to sit in (or run) a meeting for a reason. Your unique vantage point brings a different perspective to the group that is beneficial to the entire team.

Think of every meeting as an opportunity to learn something. If you are learning, the imposter has no power because you have nothing to prove to anyone else. If you continue to ask the "dumb" questions we learned in Chapter 3, every meeting you attend will give you a chance to build trust. Each interaction has the potential to increase your influence if you combine your technical expertise with the communication skills learned earlier in this book. Building trust is what Ted did that Sally did not.

Dressing powerfully also helps me minimize the imposter feeling, and many women I have spoken with agree. Clothing can be your "armor" for meetings and other work events. Dressing smartly—and for the position you want, not the one you currently have—will give you confidence.

A collared jacket or blazer is generally appropriate for most engineers attending business-casual meetings. You can tone up or down the formality based on the other pieces worn. Wearing a jacket or blazer serves two purposes: (1) It gives you an extra boost of authority. If you don't believe me, take a picture of yourself with and without a blazer and ask a friend which one looks more professional. (2) Meeting rooms are often cold, especially in air-conditioning in summer. A collared jacket or blazer keeps you warm and helps you avoid Sally's arm-crossing body language.

Now that you understand what you *should* wear, here are three things *not* to wear to work-related meetings or events:

1. Avoid pieces you have never worn before. A high-stakes meeting, presentation, or networking event is not the time to break in a new outfit or new shoes. Classic with an update is preferred over trendy in most engineering offices.

2. Avoid outfits with the potential for wardrobe malfunctions. If you need to lean over a table to point at something, can

you do this without allowing everyone at the meeting to see down your shirt? Similarly, can you pick up something dropped on the floor without flashing anyone? Can you confidently walk in your footwear?

3. Certain colors are typically more appropriate than others for meetings. Wearing a red jacket indicates power, but it can also be perceived as confrontational. Navy (my personal go-to) and gray indicate both power and trustworthiness. Choose appropriate attire colors that fit properly.

The next step to eliminate imposter syndrome is to practice a power pose right before an important meeting, event, or crucial conversation. It takes only two minutes to give yourself a powerful confidence lift! Arrive a few minutes early to the event, find the bathroom and practice there. Stand with your legs out wide and your arms either out-stretched in a "V" or with hands on your hips like Wonder Woman. Arriving early means you won't have to rush and are able to demonstrate MVT #3 calm in chaos from chapter 3. It also means you have a few minutes to greet others, which builds trust, prior to the meeting.

When you arrive at the meeting, take a seat and spread out the items you brought with you. Visually taking up space—in this case with your laptop, papers, or other items—is another version of "power posing." Sitting up straight and avoiding crossing your arms and legs as discussed in Chapter 3 also illustrate that you are engaged in the discussion around you.

When speaking, speak confidently and concisely. Silence is preferred over belaboring the point. Remind yourself of the Career Acceleration "no" list in Chapter 4, eliminating weak or unnecessary words such as "sorry", "um," "like," "you know," and "just" from your vocabulary.

We talked about the hazards of "thinking aloud" as a female leader earlier in the book. With the exception of a brainstorming meeting, force yourself to be concise when speaking. Prepare a few points you want to say prior to a meeting so that you can state them succinctly and with confidence. I have also found watching the women in TED Talks and practicing emulating their speaking styles has helped me.

You can also use the positive thinking trait you learned in Chapter 3. Some conflict is inevitable at work, and often surfaces during meetings. Look for collaborative solutions rather than placing blame, railroading others, or being overly aggressive, all of which are particularly detrimental behaviors for women. Address the situation without taking it out on the person. When people cut you off when you are speaking—and there is always at least one person who does this at virtually every meeting I have ever attended—interrupt the interrupter. Studies show that in most meetings one or two people usually dominate. Cut them off if you need to, and be aware that this behavior is a sign of a low-performing team.

Finally, and especially if you are the only woman in the room, you always have the option to say "no" to things like taking meeting notes for the team or fetching coffee. The one exception is if you are the most junior person in attendance or your manager specifically asks it of you. If you find yourself pigeonholed into this role routinely, speak up and ask to rotate the task. Alternately, request that if you are taking the notes, you would also like create the agenda and help run the next meeting.

Networking

When I bring up "networking" in the company of other engineers (and especially young engineers), I am often greeted by eye rolls and a collective groan. Isn't that something better left to the marketing experts while the engineers do the "real" work?

What do you envision when you hear the term "networking"? Happy hour? Used-car salesmen tactics? Walking into a room full of people you have never met with the expectation that you will begrudgingly swap business cards and move on with your life? A bunch of older (typically white) men on a golf course? Scrolling through your LinkedIn feed and "liking" a few posts?

These were once my preconceived notions of what "networking" meant (well, minus LinkedIn—I will admit I am old enough to remember life before LinkedIn). I thought the adage "It's not what you know, but who you know" simply didn't apply in the highly technical engineering fields. After all, who you know has nothing to do with coding or calculus.

But in a global economy where no job is truly secure, we find most of our new jobs through our networks. The U.S. Bureau of Labor Statistics (latest stats from 2012) found that 70 percent of all jobs are found through networking.[56] A 2016 LinkedIn survey of 3,000 professionals conducted by the Adler Group found this number to be even higher at 85 percent.[57] The larger your network, the more people you know. The more people you know, the better your chances for better opportunities so you can live the career of your dreams. Often all it takes is an introduction to open the door.

We live in an era of ideas and collaboration. Many of the companies that will succeed are disruptive innovators. Many of the products that are common today did not exist ten or fifteen years ago. Most of the technological advancements we will see will occur in the interface between subject areas. Online shopping and groceries are two easy-to-imagine examples that were impossible to combine in the not-so-distant past.

The ability to see your technical field from the vantage points of everyone who can be potentially impacted by your products is crucial. Expanding your network beyond your technical-proficiency areas to be as broad as the world around you gives you access to opportunities for your future self that don't currently exist.

The Internet has changed networking significantly for the better, especially if you are an introvert like me. Networking can now occur remotely. Through social media and sites like LinkedIn, we have the ability to connect with and be influenced by others around the world without leaving the room. Online connections can be made more quickly than you can attend in-person networking events. Profiles on sites such as LinkedIn enable you to quickly find common ground and connections with others, and they provide a low-stress platform for introductions to others outside your immediate network. Online networking can also increase your visibility. An article you wrote or video you created can be quickly distributed to your entire network, not simply those who were able to make it to an in-person networking event.

In-person networking is still going to be necessary at times. As discussed in Chapter 4, meeting in-person facilitates a deeper connection than meeting remotely. However, the fact that we can network online makes it possible to attend fewer and be more selective about attending in-person networking events. When we do attend, we don't need to walk into a room of strangers. You can reach out to your connections prior to an event in your area and ask if you should look for them there.

Networking isn't about sleazy tactics or "schmoozing." It is about meeting people who are different from yourself and building a relationship with them. If you look at networking as an opportunity to make new friends (and frankly who doesn't need more friends?), it can become fun if you use the tools in this chapter.

Full disclosure here: I have no marketing or sales background whatsoever. I never even took a class in college about this subject. I am terrible at remembering the names of people I have just met. Almost everything I have learned has come to me through trial and error and reading many books on the subject. I am a natural introvert who, after a long day, would rather curl up with a book than socialize. I can't even pretend to be a partier. I'm usually in bed by 10 p.m. So if I can learn to network, you can too!

Networking tool #1: Build rapport

You are buying a car. Saleswoman Ann approaches you in the lot, asks what you are looking for, and listens attentively to your response. She shows you a few vehicles in your price range and asks you what you like and dislike about each, listening more than speaking.

Always the competitive shopper, you try a second dealership. Saleswoman Mary approaches you in the lot. She sees the car you are looking at and quickly tells you that you don't want that car—you want this one with the upgrades (even though it is much more expensive and out of your budget). She then brags that she is the top seller at this dealership, that everyone loves working with her, and—by the way—don't you want to test-drive this latest model (which is still out of your budget)?

Which person are you are more likely to buy a vehicle from? Ann, who listened attentively and helped you find what you really needed? Or Mary, who was so full of herself she never stopped to ask what her customer desired?

The best networkers I know are also some of the best listeners. Like our car saleswoman Ann, when you talk to them, you are the only person in the room at that moment. They aren't checking their phone, writing a text, or glancing around to see who else (more important than you) is in the room. They show genuine interest in conversations with everyone. They don't seem to have an agenda. They aren't trying to interject while you are speaking. They listen more—and sometimes a lot more—than they talk. They often mirror your body language. You feel an instant connection to them, and you always look forward to another conversation with them.

We can build rapport with anyone if we focus less on ourselves and more on putting ourselves in the other person's shoes. It's no coincidence that the best networkers demonstrate high emotional intelligence and practice obnoxious listening. The exact same core communication traits and principles you developed in Chapters 3 and 4 can be used to expand your network.

Paul, an engineer, was talking to a potential customer at a trade show. The customer asked how Paul's newly developed product worked. Paul, who was extremely proud of his team's work, launched into a detailed technical explanation about the inner workings of the product. He didn't notice his customer's eyes glaze over with confusion at the technical explanation. When Paul finished ten minutes later, the potential customer thanked him and moved on to the next booth. Paul walked away feeling really good about his interaction, while the customer walked away feeling stupid for not understanding the technical explanation. The customer later forgot what the conversation was about, but always remembered how interacting with Paul made him feel. That potential customer purchased a similar product from one of Paul's competitors instead of Paul.

Paul broke the primary relationship-building rule: It is not about YOU. It is about the other person. The inability to put ourselves in someone else's shoes puts us on a quick route to a very small network. We can't build trust—which is required to build relationships—if we are unable to listen to or empathize with others. If we must be right all the time, we are making snap judgments during conversations that do not allow room to become an obnoxious listener.

Networking is not a competition to collect the most business cards. It's not seeking out relationships with only those whom you think can advance your career. It is building genuine relationships over time by finding common ground with the person.

You build these relationships using all the communication skills you have learned in previous chapters. Use those active listening skills, and listen more than you speak. Approach networking events with a curiosity about others and a willingness to serve others. Showing genuine interest in the person you are talking to—and following up with them after the event—is a quick path to a large network.

Dorie Clark, author and branding expert, summarizes what networking should be in her book *Stand Out Networking*: "Rightly understood, networking is a way of living your life with integrity, helping others, and benefitting in proportion to the amount you do."[58]

Networking tool #2: Be authentic

In Chapter 1, you learned about personality styles. Are you an extrovert or an introvert? Using your personality style, your networking style can be made authentic to who you are. If you are an introvert like me, this section was written to show you how this personality can build a network. I will share the things I have learned through practice that allowed me to become comfortable speaking to a roomful of strangers and meeting clients at networking events. Extroverts may also find useful tips here, however since I can't completely identify with extroverted personalities (although I love their energy!), many of these tips may not apply.

Introverts tend to have fewer, but deeper relationships. Networking often works better for them in smaller groups. If an introvert is in a large group setting, they will do well if they are able to find a smaller group with at least one person they already know. That one person would then be able to introduce them to the remainder of the group.

For introverts, networking in the traditional sense of attending events with the intent to meet complete strangers—or worse "sell" your product or company—is especially scary. Introverts may need to psych themselves up for physical networking events, and should avoid scheduling numerous meetings or networking events back-to-back to allow some quiet time between events. This quiet time allows an introvert the time to recharge and is a fundamental requirement— much like eating, sleeping, and exercising—for this personality type to function optimally. Don't apologize for this or try to keep up with your extroverted counterparts in the sales department. Instead, be well-rested prior to attending events and have a couple conversation starters prepared. Ask simple questions such as, "What brings you to this event?" and then listen attentively. If you are really nervous, step into the restroom and try some of those power poses before networking events—they really do work!

Extroverts tend to have many more, but shallower relationships. Because they recharge by being around people, they may find traditional networking fun and invigorating. Nonetheless, like introverts, it is always a good idea to come to a networking event well rested and with some basic conversation starters.

Networking in person is still the most common type. I predict this will change as those born in the Internet age become entrepreneurs and leaders. In the meantime, if you are a woman reading this book, you already have one huge networking advantage when networking in person in a male-dominated field—you will be remembered. In the sea of men's suits or polo shirts, you are easier to find in a crowd. Your name is easier to remember. I have had strangers come up to me who said, "So-and-so who is working with you told me to go introduce myself to the woman in the (enter color here) dress." Even if you attempt to be a wallflower, you are going to be remembered, so you might as well make the most of it!

Networking events are important if you want to gain influence in your field. Use five simple strategies to shine at most events.

1. Wear appropriate attire. Many events will advertise a dress code. A business event which indicates "cocktail attire" is not the time to roll out a short or tight dress, significant cleavage, or four-inch heels (unless you are comfortable in high heels). Take a cue from young women who speak at formal political events, or female business executives. Their attire is always tasteful and classic with no potential for wardrobe malfunction.

2. Be curious. Your goal is to find out about someone else using those obnoxious listening skills we discussed. Ask questions and listen more than talk. Remember, the object of networking is to get to know people, not collect as many business cards as possible.

3. Be prepared. Have a couple conversation starters that can be used in most situations. For example: "Tell me how you came to be here this evening," or, "How about those (insert local sports team here)?" If you are networking solo, look for "open" body language or other solo people to start a conversation. I am often able to strike up conversations in lines for food or the bar as well.

4. Have an exit strategy. If you find yourself ready to exit a conversation, you can excuse yourself to the restroom. You can also comment that there were a few other people you were planning to meet at this event. A good way to end the conversation is to say: "It was great talking to you. I know you are here to meet other people also, so I won't take up

any more of your time. If there is anything I can do for you, please let me know," as you hand them a business card.

5. Take notes. Do this after the event or in an unobtrusive place such as the restroom. Please don't take notes while talking! Who you met, work items discussed, personal information, and any stories shared should all be included in your notes. This information is valuable for follow-up later.

The best networking advice I can give you as an introvert who was once fearful of entering a room of strangers is that it really does get better with practice. The more you step out of your comfort zone to meet new people when networking, the more comfortable this becomes. Can you muster enough courage to show up at *one* event and start *one* conversation with a stranger? If so, you have taken the first step towards networking success, and are several steps ahead of most engineers.

Networking tool #3: Keep in touch

All that work you did to cultivate the networking mindset, attend that event, or write a blog is pointless if you don't keep in touch with your network. This is where most people falter.

Follow up after a live event should be done as soon as possible (within 24 hours). For me, this follow-up is usually completed via LinkedIn or email. You can replicate my process by sending a quick LinkedIn request (if they aren't yet a contact) or an email message. The brackets indicate where the message is customized to the reader. Keep it short: "Hi Jen, it was great to [meet you] [see you again] at the event last night and to hear about [your new project]. I'd like to add you to my LinkedIn network." This is quick and easy, and it also means you will never lose your contacts if you change jobs.

Follow up in a way that is valuable to the other person, with no immediate personal gain to yourself. Why is this important? Imagine how you would feel if someone met you at a conference and their follow-up interaction with you was, "Nice to meet you, would you buy this from me?" I would certainly feel used and unlikely to buy something from that person now or in the future. This is because the new contact asked me for something *before* building trust.

The better way is to share or give something to the person in your follow-up, even if it is only a simple thank-you. Cultivating gratitude in our networks creates trust, and the only way to receive gratitude is to give it first. See Chapter 1 if you need a reminder of why giving is required to have the career of your dreams.

The question then becomes how to follow up without allowing it to become a complete time suck. Enter the "five-minute favor." Coined by Adam Rifkin, serial entrepreneur and Fortune's 2011 best networker, this concept is one of my favorites. Adam Grant, a Wharton professor and author of the best-selling book *Give and Take*, describes why it is also one of his favorite things he learned when writing his book: "Adam Rifkin taught me that giving doesn't require becoming Mother Teresa or Mahatma Gandhi; we can all find ways of adding high value to others' lives at a low personal cost."[13]

How does this work in practice? After the initial meeting, occasionally send the person an email saying "hi" or sharing content. This should be quick: "I saw an article I thought may interest you." Sharing content without asking for anything in return builds trust. The idea is to give those in your network something tailored specifically to them without spending a lot of time. You could invite that person to a LinkedIn group. You could share an interesting article or book.

This is where being well-read and well-rounded matter as discussed earlier in the book. You name it, I've talked about it at networking events: family, music, sports, farming (not a farmer), hunting (not a hunter), politics (oh yes, I'll go there, depending on the crowd), beer brewing, places I've traveled, places I'd like to travel, pets of all sorts, and the fact that there is never a line for the ladies room at most of the events I attend.

While the follow-up after an event is important, keeping in touch semi-regularly after the initial connection is even more important to continue to build the relationships. One of the simplest ways to do that in keeping with the five-minute favors is to create a trialogue, which is a three-way conversation you create by introducing people to others. This term, coined by Alex Mandossian, founder and CEO of Marketingonline.com, is one of the most powerful ways to both help others and expand your network.[59] Being the connector between people quickly creates goodwill on many sides.

Another networking option is to host a virtual event or group. You can start a LinkedIn group and post business-related content, and you can invite those you meet at networking events to join the group (notice that once again you are connecting people). You don't have to create content; rather you can share content. As long as you are sharing valuable content, your group will associate that value with you.

Chapter 5 – What you learned

In this chapter, you learned how to make meetings and networking work for you. You learned how to overcome imposter syndrome when you may be the only woman in a meeting. You learned what to wear, how to network as an introvert, and how a five-minute favor can expand your network quickly. Most importantly, you learned how to expand your influence, which is the single-most important thing you can do to obtain expert engineer status. Influence opens doors to the best projects and career opportunities. The next chapter will show you how to use that influence to find a job that best matches your personal needs and aspirations.

Chapter 5—Career acceleration challenge

1. Clothing: Go through your work wardrobe and donate any clothing to a charity that does not meet the principals in this chapter.

2. Network: Pick a networking event to attend where you do not know anyone. Create a list of three conversation starters (that should apply to most anyone) and one follow-up question related to each prior to the event. Save these to a phone app for easy review right before the event. During the networking event, introduce yourself to at least one complete stranger and have a conversation with him or her.

3. Favor: Reach out to three people you have not spoken with in at least a month. Perform a five minute favor for each of them this week.

Chapter 6

YOUR FIRST
AND NEXT JOB

Hunting for a job can seem overwhelming. Websites abound with resume templates and tricks that claim they will score you an interview at a minimum, and likely a job. You could spend weeks researching often contradictory information related to writing a resume, the perfect way to answer common interview questions, and appropriate interview attire. You can waste a lot of time because much of the information available is not applicable to you personally or engineers in general. Alternately, you can take advantage of the hours I have spent researching, interviewing (on both sides), and hiring engineers, which I have condensed into this chapter.

Most engineers go about finding a job in the wrong way. They look for a job opening and required qualifications first, and then research the company only after they have established there is a job opening they desire. This is completely backwards. This chapter will bust that myth and show you the importance of looking at the company culture *first* so you can build your dream career. Next, you'll learn the 3 steps to getting a position at that dream company, including basic negotiation tactics. You'll also learn what to do if you find yourself in a less-than-ideal job so you are prepared when your dream opportunity becomes available.

This chapter will save you time sorting the facts from the fiction of an engineering job hunt. It provides you with an actionable "how-to" list to obtain anything from a college internship to a full-time position. It will teach you how to target a specific company and select a job that aligns with your career and life priorities as a very smart, much-in-demand engineer.

Company culture makes or breaks your dream position

Ann has graduated from college and is excited to start working for a large engineering firm in a metropolitan area. While Ann was job-hunting, she focused on the type of projects she wanted to work on to make her mark in her industry, and she chose her first job accordingly. Her first project will be very challenging technically, and she is excited to get started.

Her first week in the office, she starts to make some observations that make her uneasy. She notices that most of her coworkers have been there one year or less, yet the company is neither a start-up nor is it growing quickly. She notices her coworkers complain often, and no one seems to talk to each other except to complete the task at hand. When she asks her new coworkers if they'd like to get lunch, they comment that they usually eat lunch at their desks.

Ann's excitement for her new position quickly fades. She starts to wonder if she is not serious enough for her industry because her enthusiasm for her work is not shared by anyone else on her team. She wonders if this is how it is in all engineering jobs, and if maybe she needs to downgrade her expectations. Ann enjoys the company projects, but the gloomy, impersonal atmosphere eventually causes her to look for a new job elsewhere.

Do you think Ann would be able to achieve her potential if she continued to work at this firm? Does that answer change if her coworkers and managers genuinely care about each other and demonstrate enthusiasm for their work?

Company culture matters to your long term career success. Job postings do not often include statements such as "we value status quo," "we don't really care if you have a life outside of work", or "there's no real advancement opportunities here."

What are some things Ann could have done differently in her job search to more accurately access her potential employer before she started working there?

She could have reviewed websites like glassdoor.com for insight into the company culture. After receiving the offer, she could have requested to shadow her proposed manager for an afternoon. She could have sought out a young engineer in the company (or better yet someone who used to work there) and asked them what they liked most about working there, as well as what they most would like to see improved.

She could have reviewed the company website for clues as to the company values. Let's say Ann values giving back to the community. She would look for engineering companies that included blogs about group community service. If flexible hours, innovative solutions, or working directly with experts in her field are important, she would look for companies with these items featured on their websites. If she is planning to stay at a firm for a long time, she may want to pay close attention to companies with robust training or mentorship programs, with a special emphasis on companies that have posts demonstrating that they promote from within on their websites.

Companies–much like people—have distinct personalities. Three company personality characteristics provide valuable insight into how a firm operates, what the firm leadership values, and if it is a good candidate for your dream internship or job. Just as we know all introverted personalities are the not identical, not every firm with the same personality demonstrates the same traits. However, it is reasonable to expect that the same personality types will exhibit similar characteristics. These characteristics are firm size, special-ization, and expert status.

Engineers thrive in their careers when their own values align with the personality of the company for which they work. For example, a start-up functions differently than an established firm but will have a similar personality to other start-ups. Engineers who prefer to work under established rules, procedures, and a clear advancement path may find an established firm to be the right fit. Engineers who prefer continuous new challenges, more risk, and a flat organizational structure may find a start-up ideal. Those preferences can also change throughout your career.

Would an engineer that hates risk thrive in a start-up? Would an engineer that can't stand bureaucracy excel in an established firm? Which combination of the three company personality types is the right fit for you? Which type will allow you to reach your full potential?

Your company personality match

The three key company traits—firm size, specialization, and expert status—are indicators of a company's culture. This section will define these traits so you can determine the right match for you. Finding your ideal match will enable you to have the career you want on your own terms.

First is firm size. Many engineers have a strong preference on firm size (and they also tend to be polarized on this subject). Large firms usually have a lot of established processes in place to guide new hires or recent college graduates. They are more likely than small firms to have formal training and mentorship programs and clear advancement paths. Typically these firms are multidisciplinary firms, with industry-leading technical experts in house. They may even have research and development divisions. Due to the sheer volume of people working at large firms, as a female or minority it is more likely that you will find others similar to you in these types of firms, both at your level and in leadership positions.

The drawback of large firms tends to be the bureaucracy and office politics. In some large firms, it is also possible to become "pigeon-holed" into doing one task, especially if you become specialized in one technical area. There are many engineers who have stayed at a large firm their whole career, cross-trained across various departments, and who are very happy with their career path. There are equal numbers who moved on quickly from a large firm environment because they felt stifled by the bureaucracy and office politics.

A small organization tends to have more of a flat management structure, meaning you will likely have direct access to the firm's founder. Out of necessity, a small firm may allow you hands-on access to multiple areas of your industry that you may not get in a big firm. For example, where a large firm is likely to have people with degrees in accounting, sales, and marketing, who oversee those parts of the operations, a small firm may have an engineer who occasionally addresses some of these items. Small firms with good managers will offer a very entrepreneurial environment. If you are a young person who tends to have a lot of ideas, is self-motivated, and wants direct access to the top decision maker early in your career, a small firm may be your preference.

On the downside, very small firms are unlikely to offer much of a long-term growth path unless the current owner wants to increase the firm size. Small firms usually do not have a formal training, mentorship program, or a well-defined career advancement path. Typically the only way to advance in small firms is by managing others (a definite negative if you love the technical aspect!). It is also generally more difficult to find a small firm being led by a technical expert from whom you can learn. Lastly, it is entirely possible that if you are a woman, you will be the only one in a small firm, which makes it more challenging to develop the relationships within your firm necessary to launch your career to the next level.

Try out both types of firms in your career to see which suits you best. I started my career at a large, established firm, and I found the policies already in place helpful as I adjusted to my first job in the workforce. Moving to a smaller firm was ultimately a good decision for my values and personality, but the training, friendships, and exposure to other disciplines I received at the large firm have proved invaluable. You have to decide what is most important for you, and it is easier to do that if you have experience with both types of firms.

The second company personality trait is the specialization area. Specifically, is the firm really good at one specific thing? Or is the expertise spread across multiple things? Which type will further your career goals? If you are civil engineer, for example, your college curricula covered a wide breadth of topics. Without an internship in several of the different areas, you are not going to know which one suits your interests and talents best. It may help you to be in a multidisciplinary firm early in your career to gain exposure to the different areas without needing to job-hop. On the other hand, if you leave college knowing you want to design a particular type of robot, it will be in your best interest to find the industry-leading expert in the field and apply to work at that company.

The third company personality trait is the expert status. Do you know why a client would hire your company over another? Understanding your company's unique selling proposition is very important in any client interaction. This will also be important to you personally as you position yourself as an industry expert down the road. If you can't clearly articulate why someone would hire your firm over another, the firms' clients likely cannot either. That could potentially mean bad news for you when an economic downturn occurs.

Take a moment and write down the three company personality traits. Which characteristics are most appealing? Small or large? Specialized or multi-disciplinary? Do you prefer a firm with one expert niche or a more broad approach? Next, make a list of companies you believe would meet this criteria. Be ambitious! Pick companies with great reputations for which you would be proud to work. This is your dream company list. You will need this list in the next section.

Now you have identified your company personality match and have a dream company list, let's find out how to land that dream job!

Land your dream position

It's easy to get overwhelmed by the abundance of well-meaning advice and online information around job searching. Landing a job you love does not need to be difficult. I will break it down in three simple steps that are specific to engineers only.

Step 1 – Write a compelling resume and cover letter

You will need a resume, so start writing one. If it's your first internship or job, prospective employers know this and do not expect you to have any significant engineering experience at this point. Your resume should highlight transferable skills from any classwork, volunteer activities, engineering clubs, or part-time work relevant to the job you are seeking. Employers are looking for people who are self-motivated, driven, and collaborative. Demonstrating this on your resume will put you a step ahead of the crowd.

Clean up your online resume before you start job-hunting. Potential employers will google you. If the first thing they find is pictures of you doing questionable activities at a frat party, they will disqualify you and move to the next resume. You'll never even know this happened or have a chance to defend yourself. Google yourself, fix your profiles, and revisit your privacy settings. Create a LinkedIn profile if you do not already have one that focuses on items you would want your employer to see. If you don't already have a professional sounding email address, create one (example: yourname@gmail.com.)

The following are my top five resume tips for engineers seeking early to mid-level positions:

1. Don't copy someone else's online resume. It's OK to match their format; however, copying a resume exactly is an insult to the company looking to hire you as it assumes the person screening the resumes does not have the same access to Internet that you do. I have personally tossed resumes that appear to have been blatantly copied from a website, with changes only to names and dates and maybe a few other words. This also means you need to be honest when you describe work you have done and skills you may have because you will be asked in an interview to elaborate. Don't make up work or job responsibilities you did not do. You WILL be found out.

2. Spell-check and grammar-check. Double-check that all the contact information on your resume is valid. Details matter. I've seen numerous resumes with these types of errors. We are engineers—lack of attention to detail can cause a design to fail. If you can't take the time to make sure your resume

is error-free, why would an employer trust you to pay attention to the details on the job?

3. Gear your resume and cover letter toward the specific job you want. Create a template with your basic resume information. Then, modify it slightly to better match the job for which you are applying in each case. Similarly, each cover letter should be unique to each job to which you are applying. Cover letters should hit all major points in the hiring ad, while also addressing any company values you found during your own research.

4. First-job resumes should never exceed one page; second-job (and beyond) resumes should never exceed two pages in private industry.

5. Follow up a week or two after your send your resume. Confirm the person has received it, and let them know you are looking forward to discussing the position further.

Resumes and cover letters should be created with your audience in mind. If you were doing the hiring, would you hire yourself? Do your cover letter and resume include all the key words in each specific job application? The information you provide should be focused on why someone should hire you. Any information not specifically relevant to the job application should be eliminated.

When writing a cover letter, be specific about why you are interested in this firm and why they should be interested in hiring you. Remember, the hiring manager probably receives numerous resumes daily with the same degree and a similar GPA to yours. It's imperative that you demonstrate why they should call you instead of someone else.

Bonus tip – how to land an interview at your dream company that has no posted openings

Here's a bonus tip I have used to land interviews with a 100% success rate.

Research the companies you want to work for, find out who the hiring manager is (or if it's a small firm, go directly to the company president, CEO, or founder). Mail—and yes I mean snail mail—an unsolicited overnight package to that person containing your resume and cover letter.

Almost no one receives anything but junk in the mail anymore. Simply due to curiosity, the receiver of this package is likely to open it. And once they do, as long as you have a compelling cover letter and resume, even if they don't currently have a job open they will remember you when they do. Follow up by phone approximately one-week later to ask if they have received your information and ask when they would be available for you to come in and talk further.

Step 2 – Get an internship

Step 2 commentary: If you are already working full-time or not looking for an internship, skip directly to step 3!

Doors open when you have experience. Gain a competitive advantage by getting experience early. College graduates in engineering with relevant internships typically get multiple offers with higher starting salaries for better positions. Even if you have to do it for free, pay extra for having two apartments in the summer, live with your parents for the summer, or have to settle for a less-than-ideal internship position, obtaining an internship in your field sets you up for first-job success because it gives you an edge over other applicants who did not have a relevant internship.

In addition to the short-term advantage of resume-building, the long-term benefit of internships are even more important. It is much better to spend three months of your life in an internship trying out a specific field than it is to spend 4-6 years in college, job-hop a few times, and then realize you are in the wrong industry. Save yourself time and money by getting an internship in your field as early as possible.

In college, I worked in my parents' lab part-time one summer and did not like the isolation. That experience made me aware that this type of career would not be a good long-term prospect for me. I shudder to think of what might have happened if I had not had that experience early in my college career.

It can be difficult to get an internship at a company where you might want to work after graduation. One alternative is to ask to shadow someone for a day to get an idea of daily activities in the field. Most students have a college professor, friend, or acquaintance who can connect you with this person if you ask. Seek out someone to shadow who is doing what you would like to do in your dream position.

If you have no idea where to start, research other engineers who have your future dream job. Target thought leaders and influencers in your industry. Next, research those people (I suggest 2-3 max) and find articles, blogs, or speeches which they authored. Send an email thanking them for their fascinating insights into the industry. Ask if they would be willing to meet with you so that you can learn a little more about what they do and get their advice as to how to best get started in the industry. You will be surprised how many people will respond affirmatively to such a request.

Don't be afraid to use your network, no matter how small it may be. Many of us believe that we should obtain everything on our own merits. That is simply not how the business world works. Who you know has a lot to do with how you get started. Leverage your network, friends, parents, and anyone else you know to connect you with an internship opportunity. Your competition certainly will.

Now that you have experience, let's talk about how to ace the interview so that you get hired!

Step 3 – Interview like a Pro

Interviewing is a skill that can be practiced and developed. Some engineers are fortunate to have a knack for this. If you are anything like me however, you may need some practice. These interview skills can be used in any interview setting (such as to obtain an internship), but this section will be specifically focused on interviewing for full-time, permanent positions.

If you are like me, you will be nervous before an interview. The best defense against a case of the nerves is to be prepared. How do you prepare? You research the company at which you are planning to interview and prepare a few questions (write them down so you don't forget!). Rehearse in advance items you want to highlight on your resume and how those items meet the position requirements. You can even research the specific person who is interviewing you through LinkedIn or a Google search. Pay close attention to things you may have in common that you can use to break the ice. Examples of useful information to know is where the person is from, where they went to college, their interests, or blog posts they may have written.

We have all heard that it takes about seven seconds to make a first impression; however, Princeton researchers found that it actually takes only one-tenth of a second[60]—so make it count. On interview day, show that you value another's time by arriving approximately 15 minutes early. Be well groomed and wear appropriate attire that fits and is authentic to you. For me, that is a formal suit in gray or navy with a colorful (but not distracting) blouse for a city interview, or a classic tailored dress with a blazer for a more business-casual environment. The standard black suit is another option. It is worth noting that color psychology shows us that navy is the best color for a positive first impression[61] as it portrays trustworthiness and gravitas.

Beyond your attire, a solid handshake, eye contact, a friendly greeting, and a confident smile are the other pieces of the puzzle for a first impression. Practice these elements with a friend until they come easy to you. For many female engineers, looking someone in the eye and developing a solid handshake are the two areas that require the most practice.

During the actual interview, use the active listening skills from Chapter 3 to demonstrate how your abilities would translate to the position. Ask questions, and look for ways to flesh out additional requirements that may not be listed in the official job posting. Respond with proof as to how you meet those criteria. Consider the following example:

You: Tell me more about key traits needed for the ideal candidate for this position.

Interviewer: Well, we are looking for someone interested in this technical area, preferably someone who can jump right in with the team and hit the ground running.

You: That's great! I am very interested in this area. I even did some [insert research/class project, etc.] in this area in school. My boss at my summer internship told me that I was a fast learner. (Pause) Can you tell me more about the team and how it contributes to the overall company goals?

The key to an interview is to listen first, make sure you understand all the spoken (and unspoken) requirements of the job, and tailor your responses to those specific requirements. Questions from the interviewer like "tell me about yourself" are not meant to flesh out your life story. Rather, they are an opportunity to see how you deal with open-ended questions and if you can make a connection with the interviewer. You will ace this part if you use all the skills you practiced in the earlier chapters of this book.

Remember, the sole purpose of the interview from an employer's perspective is to figure out if you are the right fit for their position and organization. For that reason, it is usually best to practice the answer to the "tell me about yourself" question in advance. That answer should touch on your skills, why you are interested in the position, and why you are a good fit for the organization.

Alternately, if you completely blank on this question, ask the interviewer a question in return, such as, "I'm happy to tell you about myself. What would you like to know?" The answer to this question puts you in a better position to answer appropriately.

Most interviewers will ask if you have any questions at some point during the interview. Be prepared with my top three things to ask a potential employer:

1. "Describe the day-to-day responsibilities in this role." Listen attentively and ask appropriate follow-up questions. Possible follow-up questions include "Should I expect a lot of travel or overtime to be required in this position?" or "How does [enter a particular responsibility] fit into the overall company mission?"

2. "What characteristics does a stand-out candidate for this position demonstrate?" Your follow up to the interviewer's response is an explanation—using specific examples—of how you have demonstrated those characteristics. You can prepare in advance by thinking about your three best characteristics, and writing down/rehearsing a couple of sentences that illustrate each characteristic. Common responses to this question from the interviewer tend to be broad traits, such as the ability to be a team player, meet deadlines, or overcome design challenges.

3. "Tell me about how you support the professional growth of your employees." The reason for this question is so you can get a feel for the company attitude towards training, mentorship, and promotions. High performing firms—even if small—do have formal and/or informal programs.

In a first interview, do not bring up salary unless specifically asked. The goal of a first interview is to determine if you are a good fit with the company and vice versa. If the interviewer asks about your salary requirements, be prepared with a range (and never answer any questions about your previous salary as this has no bearing on what your next position should pay). You can also turn this question around and ask the interviewer what range they would typically budget for a person in this position.

Salary ranges for your field and geographic location are typically published if you know where to look. Universities will often provide this information to graduating college seniors or alumni if you ask. Websites such as Glassdoor.com allow you to search salaries using multiple criteria filters, such as job title, experience level, and physical location.

There can be huge variations in job offers by both engineering field and location. The variations do not always reflect accurate differences in the cost of living. In my industry, for example, the slightly higher offers for jobs in a metropolitan area (especially on the West Coast and in New York City) do not usually offset the cost of living there. Additionally, you can find situations where higher offers are made but the out-of-pocket costs for benefits, 401k matches, and paid days off offered result in a lower total compensation package when these are considered together with salary.

After the first interview—and especially if you receive an offer—you should ask some additional questions and/or do additional research before you make a decision. First, be sure you have met and will be compatible with your direct manager. Second, attempt to talk to as many people as possible who are currently employed there; even better, meet a female engineer who was formerly employed there for coffee one morning and pick her brain. In either case, find out what a favorite thing about working there and what one thing they would want to improve.

Consider how you feel about being associated with those who currently work there. Will you fit with the company personality and culture? Will you have the support you need to thrive in this working environment? Will you literally be the only woman in the office, the only unmarried person, or the only person with or without kids? Is there sufficient diversity in age, race, and gender? Jim Rohn, a famous business motivational speaker, has said, "You are the average of the five people you spend the most time with,[62]" so your goal at work is to surround yourself with people you would be proud to call not only coworkers but friends. Some may say that you don't need to be friends with your coworkers and I could not disagree more. Yes, you can do a good job without being friends, but you'll never reach the extraordinary success of which I know you are capable without friends at work.

Negotiation

Negotiation may be necessary in any of the previous steps. Many women, myself included, find it very uncomfortable to negotiate. Many of us have not had enough practice in life asking for what we want.

Think about negotiation like learning to swim. Would you claim to be a master swimmer based only on reading books and studying technique? We know that the best way to learn is to jump into the water. The same is true about negotiating. You can read this book (and multiple other books) about negotiating. But until you learn to ask for what you want—even knowing that "no" is a statistical likelihood—you will continue to be uncomfortable negotiating.

The statistics show that most people, regardless of gender, don't negotiate. Earnest, a lending company in San Francisco, did a recent study of more than 1,000 Americans between the ages of eighteen and forty-four. In the youngest age group (eighteen to twenty-four), they found that just 26 percent of women attempted to negotiate, while 42 percent of men negotiated. Interestingly, that gap was shown to close with age. By the time women were in their second or third jobs (between the ages of twenty-five and thirty-four), the negotiation rate increased to 43 percent versus the men's 41 percent.[63]

When women are asked why they did not negotiate, the prevalent response is that they are uncomfortable doing so, and those feelings have some validation. Pushback due to gender in negotiating is real. A 2006 study by Harvard researchers measured the impact of negotiations on job candidates. Male evaluators penalized female candidates more than male candidates for initiating negotiations while female evaluators penalized everyone who negotiated.[64]

A 2015 study of 34,000 workers in corporate America tells a similar story. Women who negotiate are disproportionately penalized for it as compared to men and are 30 percent more likely than men who negotiate to receive feedback that they are "intimidating," "too aggressive," or "bossy." Women who negotiate are 67 percent more likely to receive negative feedback than women who don't negotiate. Both genders lobby for increased compensation at similar rates (29 percent of men and 27 percent of women), but the women are less likely to be promoted than the men.[65]

The challenge here is that you could be leaving thousands of dollars on the table if you could get a higher salary and do not negotiate for it. Let's say you start with an annual salary of $50,000. If you receive a 2 percent raise every year, you will be making $88,732 after thirty years. If you upped that to a 5 percent raise, you would be making $205,807 after thirty years. That's a lot of money to leave on the table, money that could be used to fund your retirement, buy a house, or that could be saved for your kids' college education. Do you wonder what the No. 1 reason is that millennial women leave their jobs for a new one? You guessed it, to get paid more.[66]

Will all of this said, keep in mind that just because you negotiate does not mean you will be successful. The same Earnest survey showed that only 20 percent of total negotiators were actually successful in their negotiations. In my experience, you don't have much leverage to negotiate if it is your first full-time engineering job regardless of your gender. A couple years of experience combined with the certifications discussed in Chapter 2 will increase both your value to an employer and your leverage for negotiations.

If you love your current job and want a raise, ask! Be prepared to justify—in analytical terms—why you deserve it. Can you point to specific improvements to the firm that you orchestrated or to new clients you brought in? Did your excellent work create a repeat client? Did you improve an internal company process that reduces design time?

Negotiation is not just about money. Maybe your manager doesn't have the ability to pay you more (in a down year, for example), but he would be able to give you extra vacation days, the ability to work from home one day a week, or perhaps additional training. Don't sell yourself short by going into a negotiation focused only on money.

Similarly, know your own market value. You don't get a raise because you think you deserve it or because you heard the engineer sitting next to you is getting paid more. The desire to buy a house or take an exotic vacation isn't justification for a raise either. You earn a raise because you have the numbers to back up the value you bring to your employer.

Sallie Krawcheck, entrepreneur, author, and former CEO of Smith Barney, Merrill Lynch Wealth Management, and Citigroup, talks about how to negotiate as a woman in her book *Own it: The Power of Women at Work*[67]. Her top tip for those nervous about negotiation? Think about all those who would be helped by your negotiation, and frame your negotiation in a way that is a win-win. Thinking about a win-or-lose situation ("Give me a raise or I'm leaving") is a recipe for a failed negotiation.

For example: If you get a "no" on money—and remember only a small percentage of people are successful in negotiating for more money—be prepared to ask for other things that are important to you. Examples include flexible schedule, additional training, or better benefits. Be prepared to make a business case as to why these perks will benefit your employer. Make your "why" as fact-filled as possible. Think numbers and metrics when describing your performance, as opposed to the subjective "John gets to do this and I don't." Then make sure you listen to your boss' answer. If and when you receive a "no," follow up with "What skills would be valued enough to give me the promotion/perk/ability to work from home next time?"

My eldest daughter, who is nine, has this down. While shopping, she will see a toy she wants and will ask if she can get it. When I say "no," she then either asks for something smaller or less expensive, such as a candy bar, or if she REALLY wants the toy, she asks what chore she can do at home to earn the toy. She'll even use the phrase, "Let's make a deal." We both walk away from the negotiation happy.

You can apply that same principle to work. A "no" to more money may be due to things out of your boss's control. So if you get a "no" to more money, ask what you would need to do to make the "no" a "yes" next year and how success would be measured to get there. Then start documenting your progress so you can meet those metrics to earn a "yes" next year.

Jobs after a PE – choosing your track

Many engineers find themselves changing jobs and/or companies shortly after they obtain their primary certifications, such as professional engineering (PE) licensure as discussed in Chapter 2. This occurs for a number of reasons, the most common being money and growth opportunities. If you have either obtained your PE or will obtain it in the near future, it is time to proactively reconsider your priorities and values. Your priorities can and will change over time, so don't be afraid to take a new path if it adds to your skills. This is true even if others may look at it like a lateral move or even a downgrade. You career—which will last 40+ years—is better treated in today's modern labor market as a series of "app's" as opposed to a ladder. With each new "app" you obtain, you add additional tools to your skillset.

Consider the following questions: What are your next professional goals? Do you want to dive more deeply into a specific technical area? Manage others? Work directly with clients? Teach? Start your own firm? Eventually become CEO/president of your current firm? Your options are limited only by your imagination and ambition. However, fundamentally you will need to decide if you want to remain deeply technical or move into a more managerial role. Both functions require different skills and intentional practice to do well.

As your expertise in one area increases, your expertise in other areas will likely diminish. If you want to be a really good manager, your job will be to motivate and give your team the tools they need to succeed, NOT to be the hero and get the work done yourself. Many an engineer ultimately failed in management once they realized they were now managing people instead of processes.

As you consider your options, you will need to figure out where you bring the most value to your industry. What are your strengths? What are you better at and what do you enjoy more than anyone else? To maximize your potential, minimize or delegate everything else. Don't become so indispensable in a lower-level position that you cannot be promoted because no one else knows how to do what you do.

Ajit Nawalkha, entrepreneur, speaker, and business coach, cautions against spending your life in the zone of your "strong weaknesses."[68] According to Nawalkha, strong weaknesses are those things that you are good at but for which you don't have passion. Others may tell you are good at them. You may even receive promotions and accolades for them. But because they don't feed your soul, they will stall your growth because they are "comfortable" and eventually lead to burnout.

It is also important to consider your work and personal goals together. You may want to scale back on significant overtime hours to start a family or renovate a home you recently purchased. You may want a change in lifestyle by moving to another area of the country.

If you choose to become a manager, understand that the technical skills you have learned so far will not result in future success if you are unable to delegate. In Marshall Goldsmith's book *What Got You Here Won't Get You There: How Successful People Become Even More Successful*[9], he discusses the common failing of many businesses in promoting a technically excellent person to management simply because it is the only advancement path available in many firms.

Becoming an exceptional manager takes just as much practice as being excellent technically, and you can do one or the other very well or be average at both. If you are reading this book, you are well above average. Determine the path you want to take and set your goals accordingly.

Climbing to the top as a woman

Many ambitious young women have a goal of climbing to the top of their respective firms. The statistics of the number that "arrive" at that location are startlingly low: only 4.2 percent of the Fortune 500 CEOs in 2016 were female[70], which is actually down slightly from the previous two years. That 4.2 percent equates to only twenty-one women.

"It's very frustrating to see the needle move so slowly after so many years," says Naomi Sutherland, a senior partner in the diversity and inclusion practice at Los Angeles-based executive recruiter Korn Ferry. "Consciously or subconsciously, companies are still hesitant to take the risk on someone who looks different from their standard leadership profile. And when the candidate looks different and acts differently than the people around you who have been successful, it may feel like a risk to go with the woman."[71]

Most people are under the impression that the only way to get to the top is either start your own firm or job-hop. Obviously, starting your own firm guarantees you the "top job" (and all the risk and reward that comes with it). However, statistically speaking the idea of job-hopping to the top is a myth for most women. Of the Fortune 500 CEOs (male or female), only 34 percent started at the same company at which they became CEOs. When the *Harvard Business Review* studied the career paths of the specific women leading the Fortune 500 companies, they found that 70 percent of female CEOs spent more than ten years at their firm before becoming CEO. The remaining 30 percent rose up the corporate ladder at the same company for many years before making a lateral move to a different company to become CEO.[72]

For women, working their way up is a much more likely way to become CEO than for a man. Unfortunately, the same study also indicates the average length of ascension to the top for a woman (twenty-three years) is much longer than for men (fifteen years).

These statistics mean that it is critical that you find a company with a culture that will nurture you. A recent Bain survey shows that while women in entry-level jobs have ambition and confidence to reach top management in large companies that matches or exceeds that of men, at mid-career, men's ambitions and confidence stay the same, while those of women drop dramatically.[73]

Why? In the Bain survey, women at the top indicated they had to be more tenacious and committed in their rise to the top than their male counterparts. They cited a lack of female role models and a number of overt gender biases. They had to demonstrate more confidence in their abilities than their male counterparts. On her climb to the top, one woman commented: "All around us, leaders assume they know the answer to career questions for women on their teams. How often do you hear senior male leaders weighing a woman's personal life situation when considering her for something? They rarely talk about the personal life of a male candidate. Instead, men are often judged solely on objective professional criteria such as competence and experience."[71]

Making the best of a bad situation

At some point in your career, you will likely find yourself in a less-than-ideal situation. A recession may cause your industry to shed almost 30 percent of the jobs, which occurred for the construction industry in the 2007-2009 recession. You may be the victim of a bad manager, a bad client, or a bad project. Your employer may be acquired by a larger firm. A coworker may quit and you will have to make due with too much work and too few resources to accomplish the tasks until a new hire is made. During times such as these, it is important to keep in mind that an engineering career will span more than forty years, and situations like this will be temporary. They happen to everyone at some point.

When those unpleasant situations arise, although you should certainly keep a lookout for a better (new) job, you also need to find ways to make the best of the situation. One way to do this is "job crafting," which means customizing your job to make it more engaging and meaningful to your personal values. You already know how to job craft and likely do it naturally to some extent. You just need to be more intentional about it if you are in a less-than-ideal situation.

"Job crafting[74]" was coined by researchers Justin Berg, Jane Dutton, Robert Kahn, and Amy Wrzesniewski, who showed how the three ways to job craft lead to better job satisfaction. The first way is to expand or diminish the scope of your task, which includes automating it to make it less repetitive or more efficient. You automatically do this anytime you create code or a spreadsheet to increase the speed at which the task will be performed in the future.

The second is to alter relationships or interactions at work. You can avoid negative people or teach a coworker something new to deepen a relationship. I have personally found that when I am going through a stressful time at work, it is often because I have having many interactions with a new client or contractor who has a generally negative attitude. Once I recognize this, I take steps to minimize my interactions with this person. In cases where this is not feasible, I compensate by intentionally building more positive interactions elsewhere into the remainder of my day. Those are the days I make an extra effort to talk to positive coworkers, schedule lunch with friends, or make sure I take a walk over lunch.

The third way to job craft is to alter how a task is perceived. For example, in my field, checking shop drawings is fairly boring and mundane. However, it is critically important as a number of structural failures (such as the Hyatt Regency catwalk collapse) have occurred due to incorrect details on the shop drawings. Keeping the ultimate purpose of my task in mind as opposed to how mundane it may be helps me keep a positive frame of mind and be more satisfied in the work.

You can also use "job crafting" to tailor your job to include things you love to do that can expand your skills outside of the things you are required to complete. That could mean getting more involved in industry events, exploring a new technical area, or teaching others something new you have learned.

Hours, productivity, and burnout

At some point, if you are an engineer, you will be faced with a challenging deadline or set of deadlines that requires working overtime. I have never spoken with a practicing professional engineer who has not encountered this numerous times in his or her career. For a short period of time, during the "push" to a deadline, you can be more productive. However, if this becomes a chronic condition (which is certainly possible in poorly managed firms), you should consider moving on to a new position or firm. Your long hours are not making you as productive as you think.

We talked in Chapter 1 about the three pillars of wellness: fuel, sleep, and exercise. Unfortunately, many employers still don't "buy into" the importance or validity of wellness, despite the science that backs it up. Those employers may encourage unhealthy behaviors such as pulling late nights before deadlines, eating lunch at your desk, and sitting at the computer for eight, ten, or more hours each day.

Daniel Cook's research on productivity shows that working more than sixty hours a week for four weeks in a row results in lower output at the point where it continues beyond four weeks. That means that even if you go back to a "normal" forty hours after four weeks of working sixty hours, your work output is going to be less than someone else working forty-hour weeks who was not previously working sixty hours.

On his blog, Daniel Cook writes:

"In a 60 hour crunch people have a vague sense that they are doing worse, but never think that they should stop crunching. They imagine that working 40 hours a week will decrease their productivity. In fact, it will let them rest and increase their productivity.

This behavior is fascinating to observe. Zombies stumble over to their desk every morning. Tempers flare … Yet to turn back would be a betrayal."

Even more concerning, Cook found that people putting in continuous sixty-hour weeks actually *thought* they were achieving more than those working forty-hour weeks, when in fact they were *less* productive. You can see the dangerous precedent this can set: if your manager believes they are being more productive than everyone else in the office by working more hours, they will very likely expect you to do the same, even though the science proves them wrong.

You've probably experienced this in your own life. How many times have you pondered over a problem, only to magically "find the solution" when you took a break? "My best thinking" one of my friends always says, "is done when I run or when I'm in the shower afterward."

As a female engineer, you may be tempted to power through some of these situations alone. If you are like me, you may be inclined to just put your head down and work harder. This can work for a while, but it also puts you at risk for burnout down the road. We talked about how important knowing your priorities is to your career, and in situations of consistent overwork, it is important to make sure your overwork is actually needed. You should be asking your manager/boss the following questions:

1. Is this project which requires overtime the most important priority?

2. If the answer to #1 is yes, has the firm allocated enough resources to get it done properly in the timeframe given? If not, which resources can be shifted temporarily to this priority?

A 2016 survey of structural engineers found that employees who work more hours are more likely to consider leaving the profession. For each additional hour worked per week over forty, the odds of an employee considering leaving the profession were found to be 4 percent higher. This points to the tendency of people to burn out when their workload is consistently over forty hours per week.[75]

Burnout is also highly likely if you are doing project after project without recognition, which might occur in a no-growth or low-growth firm environment. If this is where you find yourself, you may want to reconsider your long-term options and look for a new position. Remember, you are a smart, hardworking engineer. You have the power to choose your own destiny.

Chapter 6 – What you learned

In this chapter, you learned how to find your first and next job. You learned how to find your company personality match and the importance of aligning your personal values with the values of your employer. You learned negotiation basics and how to make the best of a poor work situation when necessary. You learned that consistently working overtime is correlated with lower productivity and burnout, and the questions to ask your manager to make sure you stay focused on the most important work priorities so you can have a life outside of work.

You also learned some of the challenges female engineers will encounter as they climb the career ladder. The next chapter elaborates on this topic with a deeper dive into gender issues specific to the engineering profession. Why do so many female engineers drop out of the profession? Is gender discrimination and sexual harassment common for female engineers? What is the difference between discrimination and bias? Does the gender wage gap exist for engineers? What can you do to neutralize bias? These questions and more will be answered in the next chapter.

Chapter 6—Career acceleration challenge

1. Resume: Update your resume to match your current experience level. When complete, update your LinkedIn profile to match.

2. Negotiate: Successfully negotiate one thing this week. It could be calling your cell phone provider to see if they can lower your bill. It could be negotiating for Friday afternoon

off. It could be bargaining at the farmer's market. The goal is to start getting in the habit of negotiating. You have not completed this challenge if the request was immediately agreed to without discussion.

3. Delegate: Delegate one item this week to someone else on your team. If you don't have a team, delegate something to someone in your personal life. The inability to delegate is a strong indicator of burnout, so practice delegating whenever possible!

Chapter 7

UNIQUELY FEMALE: BIAS AND WHY WOMEN LEAVE ENGINEERING

Why do women leave engineering? Is there a gender wage gap in engineering? What can you do to conquer biases women encounter at work? What is the one deciding factor that determines if you will thrive or struggle in your career? This chapter will answer those questions and many more.

This chapter is both the hardest and easiest for me to write. It is easy because I've spent fifteen years (so far) working as a female engineer, and have lived many of the challenges female engineers will face. Current research and the experiences from other female engineers demonstrate that I am not alone in my struggles.

It is a hard chapter to write because it is also the chapter that makes me feel most vulnerable, and let's just say no engineer—and especially a female one—wants to be seen as vulnerable. I promised in the introduction that I would tell it like it is and give you tools to become successful. This chapter holds the key to keeping that promise.

The rate of women dropping out of engineering AFTER they enter the workforce is staggering. In tech, for example, women drop out at twice the rate of men, yet the National Center for Women & Information Technology reports that 74 percent of women in the field "love their work."[76] [77]

Is the education pipeline at fault? On the contrary, the number of women enrolled in STEM fields as a college major is increasing.[78] The National Science Foundation reports that the number of STEM degrees awarded is split nearly evenly between men and women. Specific to engineering fields, women receive 20 percent of the bachelor's degrees[79]. If this is the case, why are only 11 percent of working engineers female?

Concurrently with female engineers dropping out of the workface, the overall rate of women's workforce participation in the United States peaked in 1999 at 60 percent and has been dropping slowly but steadily since[80]. Could it be that more female engineers are opting to stay home as caregivers or start a family and the female engineer participation rate is simply matching the overall trends? Or is something else going on?

Nadya Fouad, a University of Wisconsin researcher, surveyed 5,300 women who earned engineering degrees in the last sixty years and asked those who had left to report why they had left. Her team found that female engineers who had left the field reported an unfriendly work environment that did not provide growth or advancement opportunities.[81]

A follow-up to her original 2012 study went into more detail as to where the women went when they left. Over two-thirds had left the profession to take positions in other fields either as executives or in management. Only 25 percent left to start a family.

What specifically about the "unfriendly work environment" caused the women to leave? The study found that men tended to be assigned problem-solving tasks where they could develop their analytical and technical skills. Women, on the other hand, were often assigned activities such as coordinating, writing notes, or other less technical or challenging tasks. This was especially prevalent when they were one of several engineers on a team. The women in the study cited that being unable to stretch their technical abilities and being treated differently from their male counterparts were the two primary reasons they left engineering. Examples of being treated differently included comments on their appearances and being talked down to by male superiors and colleagues.

Susan Silbey, one of the study's lead researchers from MIT, outlined the study in *Harvard Business Review* and elaborates on the findings in a 2016 *Fortune* article: "Being a manager is okay, but that's not why they [the women who participated in the study] became engineers. They like to tinker, same as the men do." [82]

The Society of Women Engineers conducted a study of 3,200 engineers across four major engineering companies (3M, Booz Allen Hamilton, Honeywell Aerospace, and United Technologies Corp.) and came to a different conclusion as to why the women left while the men stayed. Although both male and female engineers reported frustration when hierarchy and bureaucracy got in the way of their work, the study found that, while frustrated, men will continue working there, but the frustrated female will seek alternate employment options. In this particular study, that often meant leaving engineering entirely. [83]

The data, like a 2014 study by the National Center for Women & Information Technology[75] or a 2014 report by Catalyst[84], consistently show that more than half the women who enter STEM fields after college leave them within a decade, which is close to twice the frequency of their male peers in those fields. That applies even if they are in business roles.

Blatant discrimination and sexual harassment certainly exists. You don't have to look far to find stories on the numerous Uber lawsuits and the recently fired Google engineer James Damore's letter on why female engineers are inferior to men. However, these studies indicate that the incidence of harassment in most engineering firms are *not* the primary reason women leave engineering.

Where does that leave us? While it is true that there are less women than men earning engineering degrees, that does not explain why so many women drop out of engineering—at a rate twice that of men— after working for several years. Most women are not leaving engineering because of headline-provoking sexual harassment. They aren't leaving to start families either.

I don't deny that is easy to blame the attrition of female engineers on an education pipeline problem and having children. In a random (very unscientific) query of non-engineering friends and relatives as to why they thought few women are engineers, "starting a family" and "girls aren't encouraged/exposed to STEM fields as kids" were the two most commonly cited explanations.

The engineering community seems to have bought into that belief. It certainly makes us feel good to encourage a young woman's interest in engineering. Companies love to promote diversity programs and family-friendly policies to show how they are addressing this issue.

The evidence shows that although these programs are a step in the right direction, they don't address the real reason women leave engineering. Setting up a company program promoting diversity is a whole lot easier than altering the constant, subtle message of "you don't belong" displayed to anyone who does not look or act like a stereotypical engineer.

The real reason women leave is bias. It is a bias so ingrained in our culture that it is often ignored. Bias results in the unfriendly work culture, lack of technical challenges, and general career dissatisfaction that cause female engineers to leave the field.

At this moment you may be expecting the remainder of this chapter to be a man-bashing diatribe. If you are a woman you may be anticipating details of how bias is all men's fault and looking for reassurance that you are the victim. This could not be further from the truth. We *all* have bias. A female engineer or manager is just as likely to demonstrate bias as her male counterparts. Both genders continually perpetuate bias when we never stop to consider precisely how bias plays into our behavior and decisions.

This ingrained bias is an easy thing to counter if we are willing to become mindful of it. Bias comes in two categories: implicit and explicit. Explicit bias is another name for the obvious discrimination and harassment we just discussed, which makes headlines and results in lawsuits. Without the facts you have just learned, it seems the easiest target for why women leave engineering.

Implicit bias is an ingrained, subconscious bias. It's a result of societal conditioning and past experience. Because it is subconscious, it's also harder to combat, especially if we are in denial of its existence. It is implicit bias that is behind the exodus of female engineers for other industries.

Do you think you don't have any implicit biases? You are wrong, but don't take my word for it. Go to the free Harvard website *Project Implicit* (https://implicit.harvard.edu/implicit/) and take the bias test to see for yourself. Most of us are not even aware of our implicit biases. In early evolution, these kept us alive. We see a bear or a stranger and those biases told us to run away. But in modern society, many of our biases are no longer valid but they still drive our decisions.

In a study conducted at Yale in a nationwide sample of science professors, fictitious applicants John and Jennifer applied for a science laboratory manager position. Their resumes were identical accept for their names.

Participating professors rated both prospective hires' competence and likeability. The professors were additionally asked to name a starting salary and how much mentoring they would be willing to provide for the applicant if hired. The professors were told that their feedback would be shared with the student they had rated.

Regardless of the gender of the professor, the female student was viewed as both less competent and less hirable than an identically qualified male. The mean starting salary offered to the female based on this survey was $26,507.94, as compared to the male's $30,238.10. The female applicant was also offered less career mentoring. [85]

Another study by Paola Sapienza from the Kellogg School of Management at Northwestern University and Luigi Zingales from the Booth School of Business at the University of Chicago went one step further. They found that hiring practices in STEM fields favored a lower-performing man over a higher-performing woman. They also found that favoritism can be mitigated but not eliminated when hiring decisions are based on objective past performance, which resulted in the highest performer being selected 81 percent of the time. [86]

I am sure every reviewer of these resumes was convinced they were being 100 percent impartial when it came to gender and that each resume was being reviewed on merit alone. I am equally sure most engineers feel they are above bias. We are highly intelligent, educated, community-minded citizens. We like to think that we make decisions based entirely on facts. This sort of thinking is flawed. It does not match how our brain works.

The decision-making part of our brain is in the right part of our brain (yes, that's not a typo!). So although the analytical left side of the brain gathers all the data, the final say on most of our decisions comes from the right side. Emotions are required to make a decision—so much so that if you were to lose the emotional side of your brain, you could make no decisions. [87] Take this one step further, and it's easy to see that if a hiring manager says one engineer is a better cultural fit over another equally qualified candidate, implicit bias has contributed to this decision.

Admitting that everyone has bias (myself included!) is the first step to keeping women in engineering. How does implicit bias show up at work? Let me share with you a story from my first job.

In 2003, I entered the workforce. Fresh out of a highly ranked architectural engineering program, and with both a bachelor's and master's degree in hand, I moved halfway across the country to the big city of Dallas, Texas. A fellow classmate (also female) and I were beginning our careers in the structural engineering department of an *Engineering News-Record* Top 100 architecture firm.

My first day on the job, I quickly noticed we were the only female engineers in the engineering department, but I didn't think much of it. It was 2003, not 1963. My schooling had seemed entirely gender-neutral. My interests in math and science had been encouraged from a very young age, and I had never encountered bias (at least of which I was aware) in college either. Frankly, I didn't understand why university chapters such as WISE (Women in Science and Engineering) even existed.

I have always enjoyed baking and sharing my baking with others. Someone having a bad day? Bring them some cookies. Someone having a celebration? Bake a cake.

So there I was, in my first weeks in a full-time engineering position, and I brought in some homemade brownies to share at work. It wasn't at all unusual for the guys to bring in baked goods, and the only comment would be a thank-you. But when one of the senior engineers in the department tasted one of my brownies, he commented, "This is why we need women in the department."

In hindsight, I'm sure he didn't mean anything explicitly sexist by this comment. I went on to work with him on many projects (and I would add that he is a great engineer and I learned a lot from him), but his comment has stuck with me fifteen years later.

And a couple months later after that first experience with bias it happened again.

This time, at a lunch-and-learn seminar I was attending, an architectural firm principal was asked a question regarding diversity of the leadership. Specifically, he was asked why there weren't any female principals. He responded, "We did have one. She chose her family over work … At some point, you will have to choose."

I remember sneaking out of the back of the room, running to the restroom, and locking myself in a stall to cry. I had been raised to believe (and still do) that with hard work and persistence, anyone can do anything they set their mind to. What you look like should not matter, nor should your race or your gender, if you are willing to put in the work. It had never occurred to me that my gender would play into the mix. After all, most of the men in the firm had both families and successful careers. Why should a woman have to choose?

These were my first exposures to implicit bias in the workplace. Neither of these people are bad people, and I don't think they had bad intentions. They were simply telling the truth as they saw it. Such is the danger of implicit bias.

Implicit bias in the engineering workplace

The three most common implicit bias types I have encountered in the workplace are these: (1) the married woman (who either has or is presumed to someday have children); (2) the unmarried or childless worker; and (3) the worker with a stay-at-home spouse. Consider the following hypothetical scenarios:

Scenario 1: Two candidates—one male and one female—are up for hire in a small firm, both with PE credentials and both in their early thirties. Both are married—the interviewer observed this via the rings on their fingers—and have similar experience levels. The male is hired because he is the better "cultural fit" (read: he reminds the interviewer of himself at a younger age). In the back of his mind, the interviewer is wondering if the female candidate may either have or be planning to have children that would affect her work. The female is simply told the more qualified candidate was selected.

Scenario 2: John is single, and he has noticed that he is routinely asked to work late or on holidays when all his coworkers with kids are off to spend time with their families. John resents that his "free time" appears to be less valuable than others' simply because he does not have kids.

Scenario 3: Two candidates—one male with a stay-at-home spouse and kids, and one single female—are up for a promotion. Both are equally talented. The single female has been putting in an extra effort for many years. The man is also very good at his job but generally does not give extra effort. The man gets the promotion partially because—as discussed by his male superiors behind closed doors—"he has a family to support." Of course, that is not the reason the female is given for not receiving the promotion. She is simply told that he received it because of his greater rapport with clients (read: the clients look and act like the male). When she asks for specific things she can do to improve in order to be considered for a leadership position in the future, she receives feedback that is vague and not actionable. "Work harder, be less aggressive, and your people skills need work" she is told.

Do you recognize some of these biases? Do your feelings on the fairness of these scenarios change, especially in #3, if it is a woman with kids getting the promotion over a single male who has been putting in extra effort? That would smack of "reverse discrimination" to most of us, but I would bet it doesn't bother most of us as much as it should with the traditional gender roles described in scenario 3.

A less obvious case of implicit bias occurs in the following scenario. A senior manager is trying to determine which engineer should be a project manager for a new project. The senior manager expects that the new project will require some travel, and in some cases, there may not be a lot of advance notice of travel requirements. He also knows the client loves sporting events in general, especially golf. Although he has a very experienced female project manager who has expressed interest in the new project, he assigns a male project manager who is less talented but who he thinks will be a better "fit" with the client because of his golfing skills and general love of sports. The senior manager has concerns that the female project manager would not want to travel since she has young kids, even though the female engineer has never been asked how she feels about travel, nor does she routinely take unplanned time off for family reasons. To avoid hurting anyone's feelings, the senior manager tells the female engineer that although she is very qualified, the male engineer is showing "great potential" and assigns him to the project.

The challenge with most of these scenarios is that you will never know they have occurred, and most of the men (and women) making those decisions are not even aware that implicit biases are causing them to make a decision that is not based on merit. The result—especially if you find yourself the only woman in the office—is a career in which you must work harder than your male counterparts to achieve success.

What can you do about this type of bias? You can start by being aware of your own biases and consider if your treatment of others is partly based on the biases. Please know that these biases are not anyone's fault and certainly don't make you a bad person. It's simply that they have been ingrained since childhood. Ask yourself "If this person was male instead of female (or vice versa), would I see this situation differently? Would my decision change?" We will not see improvement in the retention of female or any other minority groups in engineering until everyone, and especially managers in leadership positions—are able to recognize their own biases for what they are.

The client rapport discussion is an especially tricky one. The client base in a lot of engineering industries is dominated by older white men—men who, when they married, often had a wife who stayed at home with the kids and took care of all things child and home-related. That left him free to focus all his time on work, and actually relax with his family when at home.

I have the deepest respect for anyone who stays home with the children, male or female. My mother, who stayed home with me as a child, is the kindest, most selfless person I know. However, if your client's primary interaction with a woman throughout his own life is his mother or wife in a caretaking role, it may be challenging for him to see a female engineer or businesswoman as an equal. It will be even more difficult for him to view a woman as "likeable" when compared to her male counterparts.

Researchers such as Amy Cuddy of Harvard Business School, Peter Glick of Lawrence University, and Susan Fiske of Princeton show that a competence-likeability catch 22 exists, but only for women. In fields where competence is primary (such as engineering), working mothers are viewed as less competent than women who have no children. Those same working mothers are perceived as warmer than women with no children. At the same time, when in the home context—where warmth and likeability are prized—working mothers are perceived as colder than mothers who don't work. In contrast, children have no bearing on how men are perceived.[88]

Now that you better understand implicit biases, what can you do about them?

1. Stop your own bias: Recognize gender biases in yourself and give voice to them. For example, the next time you tell a male coworker to thank his wife for baking cookies for the office, laugh and say, "I can't believe I just made that sexist comment. Thank YOU for making them." Calling yourself

out first creates awareness and gives others permission to call out other biased behavior.

2. Use humor: Use humor to call out biased statements, but always remember that the only person you can change is yourself. "How are you today, honey?" I was once greeted when I arrived on a construction site to observe the work. "Just fine, darling." I responded in a very dry tone and a raised eyebrow. That got a double take and a chuckle, and I never received that greeting (at least on this particular construction site) again.

3. Gender-neutral management: When you are managing others, always ask yourself if you would treat this person differently in the gender of the person were changed? If the answer is "yes," reconsider how you want to handle the situation. Take-charge behavior in a man that is viewed as leadership potential should not be viewed as "bossy" or "pushy" when the exact same behavior is demonstrated by a woman.

4. Use your strengths to neutralize bias: A phenomenal engineer is difficult to ignore. That's why it is imperative for you to establish and practice your strengths as discussed in earlier chapters. Remember that technical expertise we learned about in Chapter 2? Start by becoming the go-to person in that area in your company. Do you have some of the more "traditional" female characteristics, such as the ability to develop relationships and build consensus? That can potentially help you become a great project manager should you choose. Do you like to write? Write technical articles for industry publication or for your company's blog. Do you have great technical expertise but also enjoy teaching or mentoring others? Join a company mentoring program (or set one up if there isn't one), or create an online training video for your coworkers.

5. Speak up: Request interesting projects, make sure others are aware of your accomplishments, and ask for a desired promotion. When you are told "no," (notice I said *when*, not

if) find out what skills you need to develop to get a "yes" next time. Be persistent in asking for actionable feedback. When you get an email about an interesting new project or opportunity, "reply all" and let everyone know you are interested. If you see a new position that interests you but for which you are not fully qualified, go for it—your male counterparts will. In numerous studies, men went for promotions when only 50 percent qualified, while women wait until they are 75 percent or more qualified (which, for many, never comes). [89] The only way you are guaranteed to not get the project or promotion is if you don't make an attempt. Similarly, working hard but waiting for your boss to recognize how awesome you are and give you want you want is a recipe for frustration (I've been there). Your manager is not a mind-reader, nor is he or she responsible to know what is in your best interests for career progression. That is your sole responsibility.

Being a female in a male-dominated field is not for the faint of heart or one who gives up easily. You will run into—and potentially work with—others who are simply incapable of comprehending that a female engineer can be just as good or better than a male engineer.

But here's the thing: I want you to know you are not alone in that struggle. Female engineers all over the country (and world) have similar experiences to share. Our mothers, grandmothers, and great-grandmothers fought to give us the right to become whoever we want to be—including an engineer. It's up to us to actively work to eliminate bias for the next generation.

We can start by being honest with ourselves and the women around us about the bias that we do encounter. I want you to be the best engineer you can be. It is my sincere wish that you will climb to the top of your field entirely based on merit. But that doesn't match reality. We are making progress. Women at the top of their respective engineering fields—the Sheryl Sandberg's of the world—are using their influence to bring attention to the issue. But until EVERY engineer refuses to tolerate bias, we won't make significant progress. And guess what? That change starts with you and me.

I attended an engineering conference last year where, at one of the social events, a couple women had broken off into a group. One of the women was an ethnic minority living in Canada. Having never met an engineer from Canada, I said to her, "So what's it like working as a female engineer in Canada?"

The flood gates opened as she and all the women in the group started exchanging their stories. "It's really hard when you are the only one in your office," one of the women commented. "You feel left out of a lot of the informal discussions. But of course I would never say anything to the men. I work hard to be viewed as one of the 'guys.' Saying anything would only make it worse." She paused and was thoughtful for a moment before continuing. "It really doesn't help that we did have another woman in my office, but she went on maternity leave, strung everyone along that she would come back, and ultimately never came back. It's like they are assuming it's only a matter time until I leave too." She pausing, laughing. "And I don't even have a boyfriend."

What struck me about this conversation was that this was not the first time—nor the last—that I had been involved in a women-only engineering conversation. And like a broken record, every time I find myself in a group of working female engineers, the subject invariably turned to stories such as these.

Some women had stories of blatant discrimination, especially those that had worked in mines or oilfield operations. The most frequent topic of conversation centered on a feeling of not being included, a feeling that they had to constantly prove themselves in a way their male coworkers—even their less experienced male coworkers—did not, a feeling of not being able to bring their best and fullest selves to their work. The women-only engineering groups seemed to give the women permission to share their true feelings, which they felt obligated to filter in mixed-gender groups. And in almost every one of those conversations, the women commented they felt exhausted by the constant need to be less than themselves in the demanding work environment of engineering.

So I am challenging you, the readers of this book, to help me create a better support system for female engineers—a safe space, if you will—to share your stories, ask for help, and gain advice from other female engineers without the need for a gender filter. Interested? Send me an email with the request to join my closed LinkedIn group.

Having a support system is the single-largest indicator of success in your career. This is the difference between thriving and barely surviving as a female engineer. If you don't have one at work, then having an even more robust out-of-office system is crucial to your success. That support system must include your immediate family. It may include engineering friends of both genders. Friends outside engineering will help you maintain valuable perspective. Remember those mentors and champions we discussed in Chapter 2 (which you either have met or will meet through networking as discussed in Chapter 5)? They are also critical members of your support system.

Chapter 7 – What you learned

In this chapter, we learned that bias is very real but often unintentional. It has been documented in both scientific research and the stories of women just like you. It is a fact of life for women in the male-dominated engineering industry, and anyone who tells you differently is simply in denial. This chapter gave you tools to stop bias in its tracks while remaining true to yourself.

We touched on children and bias in this chapter. The next and final chapter of this book takes a look at combining life, family, and work as a female engineer. Does work-life balance exist? How does the gender wage gap factor into finding a balance? How can you have both kids and a thriving career? Read on to find out.

Chapter 7—Career acceleration challenge

1. Bias Observation: Take the bias test https://implicit.harvard.edu/implicit/. Once you are aware of your biases, name them and call them out loud when you

fall victim to them. This will help others to be more aware of their own biases. Remember, the only person you have the ability to change is yourself!

2. Community Support: Cultivate your support system by reaching out to at least one other woman in engineering by inviting her to lunch or coffee. Alternately, reach out virtually by joining my LinkedIn and Facebook groups.

3. Find a mentor: Find 1 potential mentor and set up a 15 minute meeting. To set this up, ask him or her if they'd be willing to take 15 minutes to speak with you about any advice they may have for a young engineer. Most people interested in mentoring will say "yes" to this type of request.

Chapter 8

WORK AND LIFE
AS A FEMALE ENGINEER

Work and life. Life and work. Can they be balanced? What does "balanced" really mean? Is it possible to have a thriving career and a thriving home life as a female engineer? This chapter will answer these questions from the perspective of a woman who has been there and done that (and is still doing that) in a dual-career household.

The first part of this chapter shows you how setting priorities is the key to achieving satisfaction in work and life. It discusses the origination of the gender wage gap, and how we can close it by sharing the home loads with our spouses or partners.

If you have kids (or want to have them someday), the second half of this chapter will help you from family-planning stages to navigating maternity leave and coming back to work after children. It will also show you how having kids can actually increase your productivity at work and enhance your network.

The number one question I am asked as a female engineer when it is discovered that I have three young children, is "how do you do it?" As mentioned in the introduction to this book, I have three young girls and took short (unpaid) maternity leaves for each one before returning to work. We are a dual-career household, with both my husband and I in professional careers. We don't have a nanny. We don't have a housekeeper. Our school-age kids go to public schools. I don't claim to have it all figured out, but I want to show you how you too can have a family and a fabulous engineering career if you set yourself up for success.

Work-life balance

Is work-life balance a myth? Numerous books will tell you it is. They will tell you that you can have it all, but not all at the same time. You can have kids now and focus on your career later, even as numerous studies show that our male counterparts don't need to choose. You can take off a year to travel now and find a job later. You can work part-time but forget benefits or a stable income (a.k.a. the "gig" economy). "Work-life balance" has even been re-defined to "work-life integration" in some circles.

If work-life balance is having it "all", who defines "all"? For some, "all" means running around like a chicken with your head cut off, being what you think should be the perfect friend, spouse, parent, and employee all at the same time. That results in a shotgun approach to life in which you spread yourself too thin and end up burned out and exhausted. Does this sound familiar? All too many female engineers I speak with feel this way much of the time. I have felt this way many times too.

The better way is focus. Focus on your own priorities, not the priorities others define for you. In chapter 1, you defined your priorities. Is your work and life in line with those priorities? If not, how can you make adjustments to bring it better into alignment?

At work this can be fairly straightforward. For example, I often have a priority to get a task completed within a certain timeline. I always have multiple projects going on a once, but most of the time it is fairly obvious which project is the most critical. If I were to constantly check email or allow other interruptions into my work day, my critical priority would take weeks to complete. Alternately, if I block out a couple of hours per day to work without interruption until that task is complete, that priority is quickly accomplished and I can move onto the next task.

At home, sticking to priorities can be more challenging if you are not focused on the one or two most important ones *for you*. Since engineers use so much of their decision-making brainpower at work, I advocate mimicking the most successful leaders in the world by making as many of your priorities habits as possible. I can attribute most of my weight loss to making exercise and eating healthy a habit so I didn't think about it anymore. It became like brushing my teeth and was no longer a decision I had to make. The more priorities you can build into your schedule as a habit, the happier and more satisfied with your life and career you will be.

You should also expect your priorities to change over time. Each of us has many years of living in which our definition of "all" can evolve. When I started my engineering career, my "all" included living in a big city, since I had grown up in a small town and wanted to experience city living. I was willing to commit many hours to working, but I also played equally hard. That "all" at various points in time changed to purchasing a house, running a 5K, and having kids (all while still working as an engineer). We each need to figure out the right ratio of work, family life, and play for us. It is going to vary from person to person because we are all different, but it is certain we are destined for exhaustion and burnout if we allow someone else to define "all" for us.

When you are in a committed, long-term relationship, you partner's "all's" come into play. It is critically important to discuss both your and your partner's personal and professional goals as early as possible in any potential long-term relationship. For those who choose to get married, your choice of spouse is the single most impactful decision to your career progression.

Why? Because that person is your first line of support, and if that first line is anything less than all-in on your goals, either your relationship or your goals will fail long-term. "The most important career choice you'll make is who you marry," said Sheryl Sandberg in a 2011 IGNITION conference in New York.[90] I don't know about you, but that was not mentioned in any engineering class I have ever taken.

Women in male-dominated industries marry a disproportionately high percentage of men in the same industry or another professional field (think lawyers, finance, doctors). According to the US census data, for example, 40 percent of women in construction marry a man who is also in construction. In the fields of architecture, engineering, computer science, or math, 22 percent of women marry a man in the same field.[91] Men in male-dominated fields, on the other hand, are statistically more likely to have a stay-at-home spouse, which results in some 1950s expectations in those fields as to appropriate divisions between work and home.

Put bluntly, if the management at your employer always had a spouse at home to take care of everything related to the home, including the children, you can expect them to have difficulty understanding why you would need off work for any of those activities. They won't even think that view is biased toward women. It is simply the truth in their own experience.

Traditionally, engineers have worked longer than a forty-hour week, and many engineering firms encourage this culture. Face time and "busyness" are valued in many engineering firms. The person who comes in early and leaves late must be getting the most work done, right?

Wrong. The cultural belief that busyness is productive is a myth. Science shows that constant work without a break actually makes you less productive.[92] As we discussed in Chapter 5, it only gives the illusion of being more productive. Busyness leads to lack of innovation because the brain cannot be creative or focused when it is constantly "doing." The US Department of Labor's Construction Industry's productivity chart is one prime example of this. It shows a productivity decline since the 1970s, even as the hours worked have risen.[93]

The brain is a muscle, and just like any other, it requires a rest. Would you ask someone who just completed a marathon to now run a sprint? Why then do we think we can accomplish more in twelve hours than we could in eight? And how can we achieve balance in this environment?

Let's look at this in a different way. Can working more hours (and presumably making more money) lead to balance? After all, if we are making more money, we can balance our lives by hiring a lot of the home functions out, right? Think housekeepers, nannies, grocery delivery, and eating out.

Not so fast. We discussed in Chapter 6 that there is a gender pay gap—even when controlled for other factors, such as time off for kids. It's worth repeating. This gap exists even when controlled for everything else. There's a gap for a single woman. There's a gap for a woman who is married and never intends to have children. There's a gap for women with children whose husband stays at home with the kids. If you are female, there is a gap.

That gap can't be explained away "because she has children." Overall, women earn seventy-six cents for every dollar earned by men. As with any statistic, the numbers tell only part of the story, but no matter how it is sliced, that pay gap does exist. [94]

Academic studies show that married professors get ahead, but only if they are male. This is true even in female-dominated areas (think English professors)[95]. Move to engineering private practice, and we see that women are promoted more slowly and still make less money. A 2016 study of structural engineers found that for full-time employees with children, men with fourteen to seventeen years of experience made $9,700 more per year than women with the exact same amount of experience. Men with eighteen to twenty years of experience made $43,400 more per year than women.[73]

We even see the gender wage gap in traditionally women-dominated industries. Male nurses make $5,000 more on average than female nurses. When we consider those with PhDs across all industries, we see this group has one of the largest gaps at more than 5 percent for similar work.[96] Graduates of Ivy League schools report the second-highest controlled gap at 4 percent. Architecture and engineering professionals (my field) have a 1.7 percent gap.

Yet even with the evidence that proves the prevalence of the gap, almost half of the employees and 57 percent of the employers surveyed reported that they believe there is no gap. We have a profession in pay gap denial. I suspect this is because, as long as we are in denial, we won't be forced to come to terms with the hard truth that this means one's achievements may be based on something less than merit.

Sharing the home load – the PEACE method

Fathers now see caring for children nearly as crucial to their identity as mothers see it. A 2015 Pew study found that the amount of time fathers reported spending on childcare is triple that from 1965.[97] Fathers self-reported spending seven hours a week on childcare and nine hours a week on household chores. Mothers reported spending an average of about fifteen hours a week on childcare and eighteen hours a week on housework. That means that mothers spend an average of five more *weeks* a year than fathers on childcare and housework.

Finding balance is a challenge for both male and female parents, evidenced by the same study that found that 50 percent of men and 60 percent of women reported that it is very difficult to balance work and family life.

Early discussions with your partner about role expectations—preferably long before you plan to start a family—are important. In the modern age, most highly educated professional spouses will say that they expect to share an equal load, but the definition of "equal" is very likely to be different between spouses.

We have been conditioned from childhood to have particular expectations regarding role division by gender. Without introspection, it is unlikely you are aware of your own expectations, and it is likely you will assume your partner's expectations match yours.

Imagine large family gatherings on both sides of the family, such as the Thanksgiving meal. Who cooks the meal? Who cleans up? Is it equitable by gender? If not, both of you likely have some implicit bias toward gender roles in the home. If for example, the men typically "relax" after the meal, watching a football game, it is likely a male spouse will think he has shared an equal load if he has helped clear the table while the other men were relaxing. It won't even occur to him that his wife, who is now doing the dishes, would have liked to sit down too. Lack of clear expectations can lead to long-term resentment.

Did your partner have a stay-at-home parent? If so, extra discussions may be needed. The partner with the stay-at-home parent may not have been exposed to everything that the stay-at-home parent did while they were at school. That results in unrealistic views of precisely how dinner appeared on the table every evening (grocery shopping in addition to prep work), the planning of numerous family events, and how the house was magically cleaned and laundry done when that partner arrived home.

If you struggle with equally distributing the work it takes to run your home and/or take care of your child(ren), try the "PEACE" method to share the load. While it won't lead to total peace in your house, it will alleviate a lot of the pain by exposing expectations. PEACE stands for Plan, Enable, Adapt, Care, and Every day.

Planning means that you discuss expectations for domestic tasks up front and divvy them up accordingly. Set up ground rules as to how something should be done and who should do it. Some tasks that everyone hates are alternated. For me, that is cleaning bathrooms. For you, it may be grooming a pet. Set up a schedule of tasks and when they need to be completed. For example, trash goes out for me on Thursday nights, the dishwasher gets loaded every night, etc. Divide up tasks by the time it takes to complete them, not by the quantity. In my house, mowing grass and taking out the trash are not equal tasks, but mowing the grass and doing laundry are pretty close. The goal is to make the total time as equal as possible.

As part of the planning stage, it can be valuable to incorporate a family meeting once a week. Kids old enough to help are also assigned tasks. A two-year-old can feed the cat if she is reminded. A six-year-old can put school snacks in backpacks for the next day. An eight-year-old can help fold laundry. Everyone can be responsible for assisting with a once-a-week house pickup and vacuuming. And they can all put their socks away when laundry is done.

Enable means that you set yourself up for success, largely by realizing to let the little things go. In our house, that means that whoever is NOT doing a task can't complain the other is not doing it right unless it is a matter of safety. It means having a spot for things in the house to enable putting things away to become a habit. The keys have a key hanger right next to the door. We designated one room of the house as a "toy room", and allow the kids to make as much of a mess as they desire until clean-up day, which has greatly reduced the amount of stress in our house. I stopped stepping on toys everywhere (and stopped yelling at the kids as much to pick them up). Enabling also means that we batch errand runs. For example, grocery shopping can occur between drop-off and pickup for one of the kids' events.

Adapt means that we do two things. First, we accept that things don't always go according to plan. There will be illnesses, a last-minute business meeting scheduled, and work or home emergencies that may cause chaos. This means we need to plan well enough to account for some of these contingencies (more on that in the "kids and work" section of this chapter). Second, we have to be flexible; after all, flexibility is a required life skill. Choose to leave enough space in your schedules so that when one thing doesn't go as planned, it does not create a domino effect with other activities.

Care requires you to remember that your primary task as a spouse or parent is to care for each other. Being present is more important than checking something off the house "chores" list. It is prioritizing time with your spouse and kids in the evening above a spotless, dust-free house. Time for play is required for healthy families. Keep it simple. Perhaps everyone forgoes chores on Friday nights in favor of pizza and a movie instead.

Every day means that, in addition to dividing up weekly chores by total time, critical daily chores are divided up evenly also. These chores are assigned to household members, take approximately the same amount of time, and will be done concurrently. Everyone in the household—with rare exception for events or work travel—is responsible for completing these chores every evening. What does this look like? If you have a pet, that means if someone is walking the pet after work, others are getting dinner ready. After dinner, one spouse may be cleaning up from dinner, while the other is helping the kids complete their homework and pack lunches and bags for the next day. The goal is for all household members—including and especially children—to have both a shared sense of work and a shared sense of being able to relax when those tasks are complete.

The family meeting

The family meeting is an important part of keeping the PEACE. In some families, it happens organically, and there is no need for a formal meeting. In other families, an informal meeting is held every night as the family eats together. You don't need a lot of time to hold one, a quick twenty minutes once a week will get everyone on the same page and eliminate a lot of hassles for the week.

If you opt for a formal meeting or are trying this for the first time, try my quick-start tips:

1. Pick a consistent day/time for the meeting. Sunday night works well for a lot of families.

2. Eliminate electronic devices. No cell phones, iPad, laptops, etc. may be used in this meeting EXCEPT as required to reference a calendar for upcoming events in No. 5.

3. Divvy up any "must-do" chores for the week during the *first five minutes*. "Must-do" chores include items that would result in people being hungry (e.g., grocery shopping), naked (e.g., laundry), or result in general icky-ness (if dishes don't get done at least every other night, mice or fruit flies may appear). Kids are included and assigned chores that are appropriate for their ages.

4. Talk about family goals (either personal or professional) for the month during *the next ten minutes*. Talk about vacations you want to take together and make plans for them (you can assign tasks for this as well, for example, "research vacation locations").

5. Discuss any "critical" meetings or events this week in *the last five minutes*. This should include any important business meetings with the potential to run late or start early and kids' events that require family attendance. Put backup plans in place if needed in advance.

Critical meeting tip: If one or both spouses travel for work, plan for backup people in advance (sometimes that takes multiple calls). Either don't schedule early morning or end-of-day meetings (my personal preference), or make sure someone else is available to drop off or pick up the kids at daycare/school if a meeting runs late.

Planning a family

Numerous books, blogs, and Internet libraries exist about family planning and what to know when you are pregnant. The purpose of this section is not to rehash things you can find elsewhere. Rather, it is to give you some tools for situations you may encounter specific to the engineering fields that I wish I had known before starting my own family. Read on for some secret—and some not-so-secret—tips to help you successfully start your family while continuing an upward trajectory in your engineering career.

Today, a lot of women assume that employers will be reasonable when it comes to pregnancy and family leave and that they cannot be fired for being pregnant. That's not necessarily true, which makes planning for your family all the more important.

It is fairly well-known that the Family and Medical Leave Act (FMLA) mandates that you can't be discriminated against for becoming pregnant or having a baby. This act allows you to take a short leave (up to twelve weeks) and return to the same job, assuming you have met some minimum requirements. For example, in most states you need to have worked at a job for at least a year, which means if you change jobs when you are pregnant, you won't be covered and will need to negotiate this before starting a new job.

Although a growing number of states, such as California, New Jersey, and Rhode Island, offer paid maternity leave, the reality is that fewer than 40 percent of workers in the United States qualify for FMLA and only 14 percent have access to paid leave through their employers.[98] Most of the workers that are covered by FMLA work at a small number of very large firms. The US Department of Labor reports that 89 percent of American businesses are not covered by FMLA[99].

Besides the number of workers, FMLA has a number of other exceptions. For example, you are only covered you if you work in an office location with fifty or more employees within a seventy-five-mile radius. If you work for a small business with less than 50 people, you are definitely not covered. You could potentially not be covered if you work in a branch office of less than 50 people in a large organization. In addition, there are a number of at-will employment states that allow either you or your employer to part ways for any reason whatsoever, up to and including being pregnant or wanting to take time off to give birth and bond with your little one.

Much has been written about the lack of family leave in the United States. We are the only developed country in the world without paid parental leave, on par with countries such as Swaziland, Lesotho, and Papua New Guinea.[100] However, the purpose of this book is not to argue the pros and cons of paid parental leave. Rather, it is to make you aware of the challenges you may face in advance of starting a family.

I don't say this to scare you or make you think that you can't have a family and be a successful engineer. Many successful engineering firms recognize their employees are their greatest asset. From a strictly financial basis, it costs much more to train a new engineer than it does to retain an experienced one. Most employers see it as a win-win to work with employees who have proven themselves in order to craft a short personalized leave policy. In my professional circles, this leave seems to range from eight to twelve weeks, depending on the situation.

With my first pregnancy, I had no idea I was not covered by FMLA. I work for a small employer and was the first female engineer in the office to ever take maternity leave. There wasn't a formal plan, so we crafted an informal one for each of my three children. I am proof that this can be done and was fortunate to work in an accommodating family-friendly environment. However, if you are not so fortunate, it is better to be prepared than to be dependent on the benevolence of your employer.

Understanding parental leave policies at engineering firms

Prior to becoming pregnant, learn about the leave policy at your place of work. Does one exist? Can both parents use it? This is especially important if—like me—you will be the trailblazer for establishing a parental-leave policy in your office. This section assumes you are planning to continue working at the same firm after a baby.

Consider the following questions:

1. Does maternity or parental leave exist? If so, how is it structured? Has the policy actually been used by both men and women, and if so, how much time did they take off? Your goal is to determine if a policy exists, and any unofficial "rules" around using it if one does exist. Initially, this is not the time to talk to HR. Rather, talk to any new parents. For example, there are firms where paternity leave exists, but there is an unspoken rule that men don't take more than one week off except for extreme complications.

2. What and how much does your healthcare cover for prenatal check-ups and delivering the baby? Do you need additional coverage? How much can you expect to pay out of pocket? Call your healthcare provider directly to find out (they are required by law to keep this inquiry confidential). There are companies like Aflac that have maternity policies you can buy on top of your healthcare insurance that will provide partial cost assistance in the event your baby needs to go to the NICU (neonatal intensive care unit). However, these policies typically need to be in place at least one year prior to the child's birth. Similarly, switching jobs less than 1 year prior to having a child may result in additional cost complexities or non-coverage. Out-of-pocket and deductible costs can also vary greatly; it will cost you several thousand dollars out-of-pocket just for a non-complicated hospital delivery.

3. What is your company culture? We have talked about how important this is in previous chapters. You will find that, for example, that despite technology, a lot of engineering firms still put a lot of emphasis on face time. Infants require a lot of doctors' appointments and can get sick often, particularly if they are enrolled in a childcare center. Does your company allow you to work from home a couple days a week? Is travel required constantly with your job? Will your current schedule work for you after your child is born?

Now that you understand maternity leave plans and the initial costs (hidden and actual) of starting a family, it's time to start establishing the most critical component to thriving as an engineer with a family: your support network.

Establish a family-friendly support network

Female engineers with strong support networks will thrive. Women with weak or non-existent support networks will struggle and eventually drop out of the field entirely. This is such a crucial part of starting a family that it cannot be overemphasized.

Every question you could possibly have about raising children has been answered successfully by someone in your community. For every child-rearing difficulty you will encounter, someone has found a solution. All children are certainly unique, but there are established ways to raise healthy, happy children with working parents. All you have to do is seek out and surround yourself with others who will support your work and your family. Most importantly, you must be willing to give as much as you receive.

Establish as much of your support network as you can in advance of the baby's arrival. In my case, it meant securing a well-paying job at a family-friendly firm in close proximity to my family support network (aka the grandparents) and becoming actively involved with other parents with kids of similar ages once my children were born.

What does that support network look like? The following are examples of the caregiving support categories most successful working parents (not just engineers) have. These are listed in no order of importance:

1. Paid childcare or after-school care: Examples include a daycare center for kids younger than school-age, or after-school care associated with a school. Be prepared for sticker shock—in many locations daycare for an infant will cost more per month than your rent or mortgage.

2. Family: Relatives by blood. One caution here—Do not assume a relative (such as your child's grandparents) will be either willing or able to watch your children all the time while you work. This can be very overwhelming to some grandparents and will change the dynamic between all of you—you and your parents and your kids. Things have also changed a bit since your parents last took care of an infant. Grandparents may or may not be open to current sleeping, eating, and discipline recommendations, and Grandma isn't as much fun to her grandchildren on vacation or visits if she also watches the kids full-time (including being the disciplinarian if needed) while you are at work.

3. Other parents or friends: This includes people you can meet at daycare, school, and church (if you have a spiritual leaning). Typically for us this includes a lot of parents with kids in the same schools/grades as ours, which allows for carpools to events, after-school activities, and the ability to trade off snow days and in-service days. The key here is to make sure the trade-off is reciprocated. Stay-at-home moms have plenty of work to do; if you ask one for help, make sure you reciprocate when you can.

4. Paid evening/weekend babysitters: We typically use these for "date night," especially if we are going to be out late.

The pregnant engineer

The first days of pregnancy can be very exciting and scary at the same time. You may be wondering when you should tell your coworkers or boss about your pregnancy, if there are any work conditions you should avoid, and how to handle morning sickness at work. You may be the only woman—let alone pregnant woman—in your engineering office. There are many other resources available that explain the physical changes in pregnancy, so this won't be our focus. Instead, we will target the lesser-known art of navigating a male-dominated profession while pregnant.

When should you tell your coworkers or boss you are expecting? Unless you have a medical reason to do so, many women prefer to avoid telling anyone at work until the first trimester has passed. A lot of women don't gain any weight during that time, and for those like me that do, it's usually no more than 5-10 lbs. which is easy to cover up with clothing. The primary reason to wait is because the first trimester is also at a higher risk for miscarriage. Imagine how difficult it would be for everyone involved if you had to explain that you were no longer pregnant. Once the first trimester passes and the risk decreases, it will be time to let others at work know.

Everyone knows about morning sickness. If you do get sick (which typically happens during weeks eight to twelve), find a ritual that works for you. For some, it is ginger tea. For me, it was keeping a box of plain crackers at my desk. Unless you are sick during a meeting with clients or out on a work site, the changes in your behavior are unlikely to be chalked up to pregnancy. People pay less attention than you think, especially if they are men and have not been around pregnant women. I had a coworker in the cubicle next to me who experienced extreme nausea, and I still did not suspect she was pregnant until she told us in the second trimester.

When you do tell your boss or manager that you are expecting, be prepared with a plan. Make sure you have specific dates you expect to be off work, dates you expect to return, and how you will document current projects in order for a smooth transition to other staff while you are out. Five to six months (assuming you disclose near the beginning of the second trimester) should be more than enough time for your firm to hire a temp or add another person to your projects to get up to speed as needed.

A pregnant engineer is a rare creature. Some people will not change how they interact with you in the least. Others may seem to think that your brain doesn't work when pregnant. Let me assure you it still functions fine; some of my most focused work has been done while pregnant. As a structural engineer who is mostly an office worker, part of my job responsibilities include infrequent construction site observations. I have performed these while pregnant, including climbing an occasional ladder. A little common sense goes a long way—I did what I was comfortable doing, and encourage you to do the same.

A pregnant woman should talk to her doctor regarding work conditions if they are hazardous. Tell your boss in advance if there are any job functions you will not be able to perform when pregnant. Many female engineers like me—who are predominately office workers and have uncomplicated pregnancies—will see little change in what they can accomplish at work when pregnant. Other women may have complications or simply be exhausted and need to cut back on travel or hours. No two women or pregnancies are the same, and I encourage you not to assume your capabilities in advance of being pregnant.

Finally, a word on travel: Do not expect to be able to fly during your third trimester. Different airlines have different requirements, but most have a cutoff somewhere around thirty weeks. The same will go for long road trips near your due date, so make this a part of your plan if needed.

Returning to work after baby

My oldest child, Claire, was born on Christmas Day in 2008. The great recession was starting to hit the commercial construction industry at the time. My husband, a civil engineer, was laid off from his job in January 2009, which meant I needed to return to work earlier than expected to pay the bills.

My first week back, I was asked to travel to an important client meeting several hours away. I was still breastfeeding the baby and had never used a pump before.

This is how I found myself in a very painful situation when the meeting lasted six hours with no significant breaks. Because I was traveling with someone else in the office, ten hours passed between when I last fed Claire that morning and when I was able to use my (very loud, large, rented, hospital-grade) breast pump—in a public restroom, no less.

I learned my first back-to-work with baby lesson that day: practice with a pump before you use it. I also learned that I should not be shy about excusing myself from a meeting for a long bathroom break. It took me a second child before I further learned to use a small, quiet, portable pump that fit easily in most handbags.

There are literally thousands of books, blogs, and advice out there for women returning to work after having a child, and most highly recommend making your first week back a partial week. Specifically, start back on a Wednesday if starting back full time or negotiate a half-day full week schedule for the first week. I heartily endorse that recommendation. Adjusting to a new schedule and care givers is hard on both the baby and yourself, which is why a gradual build-up to a full "standard" work week is best if possible.

During those first exhausting weeks back at work, self-care and baby care must be the highest priority. Delegate everything else where you can. Go to bed when you put the baby to bed in the evening. Alternate "night duty" with your partner so that every night one of you gets six to eight hours of continuous sleep. If you are breastfeeding, advance planning will be needed but is worth it. Pump in advance if needed, or have your spouse use formula at night. You can use both (I have). Tap a grandparent or babysitter for an occasional job during the middle of the day on a weekend so that both you and your partner can take a long nap or just enjoy some baby-free time.

The following are my top five "learned-the-hard-way tips" for returning to work and the first three months back. I am sharing them with you in hopes that you can learn from my mistakes, and also understand how completely normal your experiences are. Guilt the first days and weeks back to work? This should be expected. Feeling exhausted most of the time? Also expected and usual for all new parents. You may feel alone and isolated, especially if there aren't other women or parents of young children in your office. Remember to be kind to yourself and your spouse during these days. The house doesn't need to be spotless and frequent carryout meals are OK.

1. Breast-feeding and work: You will be inundated with the whole "breast is best" thing in prenatal classes, so it's important to get over any judgment (from yourself or anyone else) regarding how the baby eats. As someone who does not respond well to a pump (and I went through several high-grade ones), I beat myself up a LOT about this with my first child. The only private, non-bathroom space where I could pump at work with my first child was a janitor's closet right next to the kitchen area. With the size of my pump and how noisy it was, I ended up giving up on pumping/breastfeeding her about a month after I went back to work because I did not realize I could breastfeed "part-time." I accidentally found out with my second child that I could feed her in the morning, stop feeding her while I was working (8:30 a.m. to 5:00 p.m.), pump once at lunch, and then feed her in the evening. Our second child had formula during the day but still got the benefit of breastmilk when I was with her. We used this method for child #2 and child #3. We noticed that the two younger children who had been fed a full year were sick substantially less often in daycare than the oldest one was at the same ages.

2. Travel: Cut back on significant travel if possible until the baby is at least six months old. That is about the time all three of mine started to routinely sleep through the night or (at most) woke up once during the night but immediately went back to sleep. Traveling as a zombie is no fun.

3. Exercise: Make an effort to incorporate some exercise, no matter how small the amount. I used to grab the baby carrier as soon as I got home, strap the baby into it, and go for a quick walk. We both loved the snuggle time, and I got some exercise. Since dinner came after the walk, the baby was unlikely to fall asleep on our walk.

4. Adult time: Don't forget about your spouse or partner when you return to work. After a month of adjusting to the new schedule, set up a date night or afternoon if that works better so that you can have a few hours of work-free adult time.

5. Have a backup plan: I always seem to get an emergency ("running a fever, come pick her up right now!") call when I am on my way to a client meeting. Talk to your spouse about who will do pickup if needed, and if your partner is not available, have another backup.

Kids can help your career

It is well-known that having children increases a father's earnings. Dubbed the "fatherhood bonus," researcher Michelle Budig from the University of Massachusetts found that men's earnings increased by an average of more than 6 percent when they had children. In contrast, women's earnings decreased 4 percent for *each* child she had. The dad bonus is most prevalent for white men and professional workers. The mom penalty is worst for women in lower economic brackets. The study speculated that the reason for this can be at least partially attributed to the division of labor at home. With each subsequent child, this study found that women spent more time on childcare and home chores. Men, on the other hand, tended to maintain the total time spent which kids. More children for them meant spending less time with each one. [101]

The wage gap research—for all women—discussed earlier in this chapter in combination with the motherhood penalty illustrate that much of the difference can be attributed to hours spent on home chores or childcare. If you equalized those hours with your spouse or partner by using the PEACE method in combination with all the other skills you have learned in this book, you will maximize your earnings.

Wages aside, there are some surprising and unintended consequences of being a parent. We've all been told that growth begins at the edge of our comfort zone, but we don't often apply this to parenting or how growth in our parenting abilities can readily translate to work. Approach parenting as a chance to learn new things, and you will find the top five ways having children can help your career:

1. High-definition priorities: Having kids forces you to better define your priorities and more importantly stick to them. Having priorities means you become better at setting boundaries, which ultimately results in a happier, more productive life. Most people—and especially the women like me who have been conditioned by society to people-please—do a poor job of setting boundaries and saying "no." And yes, it is possible to say "no" at work without being negative. For example, if you are asked to take on a new project and you already have a full plate, you can say, "I would love to take on a new project, but my plate is really full right now. Which of my other projects can be put on the back burner or delegated to someone else so that I can take care of this one?"

   Before kids, you had the ability to say "yes" to lots of things without considering the consequences. It did not matter if you ate dinner late or missed a sports event. Kids—and the additional schedule constraints involved—force you to weigh everything against why you are doing it and what is most important. If it is not important, ditch it. If someone else can do it, delegate it. If it is important and you must do it, schedule it into your calendar so that it gets done!

2. Organizational super-powers: Organizational skills improve to epic proportions when children are involved due to necessity. There is nothing quite like trying to get two working parents and multiple kids out the door in the morning. You'll find pre-planning *everything* and breaking

down large tasks into easily accomplished action items becomes second nature. Our evening routine is case in point—all backpacks and lunches are packed, and clothing laid out for the next day prior to going to bed.

Many dual-career parents demonstrate extremely strong organizational skills, which can often translate to work in the ability to juggle multiple projects at once and make faster decisions with less data. That's not to say that non-parents are not organized or slower decision makers. Rather, organization is a skill like any other that can be developed. Parenthood requires constant practice by necessity, and someone who is constantly practicing a certain skill will always improve more quickly than someone who does not practice.

3. Self-Discipline: Kids in your house improve self-discipline by helping you build healthy habits. If I want my kids to have healthy habits, they need to see me demonstrating those habits. If I don't want them sitting in front of the TV all day on the weekends, overindulging in sugary beverages, and eating pizza or takeout every night, that means the adults in the house can't do that either. (Did I mention I lost eighty pounds between my second and third child?)

4. Emotional intelligence expansion: Having kids improves your emotional intelligence. Empathy develops when you realize how completely useless it is to tell a 3 year old to suck it up or "calm down" when upset (that tactic is equally ineffective for adults). Many women find that their long-dormant negotiation skills are a force to be reckoned with when it comes to advocating for their children. On a personal level, my patience levels and my ability to tolerate difficult clients and personality types have become much more effective because I use this "muscle" every day with my kids in a way I never did prior. This develops skills like patiently explaining something for the fifth time, reassessing and stating very clear expectations, and staying calm when someone is yelling at you, crying, or otherwise being unreasonable. These skills are very, very handy in most

corporate environments. Who knew Chapter 3's MVT #3 of Calm in Chaos would be developed here?

5. Network expansion: Kids expand your network dramatically. Prior to kids, I spent a lot a time with the same group of friends. There were deep friendships, but the network was small. After kids, the network expanded into the parents of all the kids at daycare, at school, at dance class, at swimming, at tennis, at scouting, at church, at volunteering associated with any of the above groups ... you get the idea. The world expanded to people I would not have met otherwise if I did not have kids.

Chapter 8 – What you learned

In this chapter, we have learned that balance is in the eye of the beholder. You learned how you too can have both a family and a satisfying career as an engineer by prioritizing, planning, and getting help from your support network. You learned that the gender wage gap exists and the motherhood penalty exists and how they can be minimized by sharing the workload at home through the PEACE method. You also learned the basics of navigating pregnancy and the going back to work after baby. Finally, you learned that having children can help you become more organized, disciplined, and expand your network.

Chapter 8—Career acceleration challenge

1. Hold a family meeting: Even if you don't have kids, try out a family meeting this week and see how it feels.

2. Leave policy: Educate yourself on your company's parental policy.

3. Support System: Evaluate your current support system. Is it adequate or do you need to make some friends? If you need

to make some friends, pick one family-related group to join this week.

Conclusion

CHART YOUR

OWN COURSE

Now it's your turn. It's time to take charge of your career so that you can live your dream life. This book has given you the tools. It is up to you to study, practice, and apply them.

In Chapter 1 you learned the leader's mindset and strategy. You learned how to determine your strengths and values. You imagined what success looks like for you, and learned secrets to success as a female engineer.

Chapter 2 taught you how to become an engineering expert so that you have the leverage to achieve the success you defined in Chapter 1. You learned that experts constantly expand their knowledge, share it to others, and seek out learning and growth opportunities. You learned that everyone experiences imposter syndrome and discovered tools to give you the confidence to silence that inner critic. You learned the importance of seeking out mentors.

In chapter 3 you learned that engineering leaders have excellent communication skills. You practiced the most valuable communication traits (MVT's) of obnoxious listening, positive thinking, and staying calm in a chaotic world. You learned actionable ways to develop those skills so you can quickly earn promotions, more money, and have your pick of the best projects.

Chapter 4 taught you how apply the leadership communication mindsets from chapter three. It provided methods to approach engineering-work-specific communication tasks, such as technical writing and speaking, to make sure your expert message is heard and acted upon. You learned that communication skills are necessary to build the trust of those around you, which is essential to becoming a leading engineer.

In Chapter 5 you learned how to use the skills learned in the previous chapters for meetings and networking—even if you currently hate talking to strangers. You learned how to best present yourself, stand out as a woman in positive way, and methods to silence imposter syndrome. You learned how to expand your influence by making networking work for your personality type.

Chapter 6 showed you how to find your dream job. You learned the importance of aligning your personal values with the values of your employer. You learned how to craft a resume, interview, and negotiate. You discovered that constantly working overtime is correlated with lower productivity and burnout, and how to use job-crafting to maximize your satisfaction at work.

In Chapter 7 we tackled facts and myths surrounding gender bias and women in the engineering workforce. You learned the number one indicator of career success is having a strong support system, including family, friends, work colleagues, peers, and mentors. You learned that bias is very real but often unintentional and that each of us has bias. I shared a number of tools I have successfully used in my 15 years working as an engineer to combat bias while remaining true to myself.

Chapter 8 showed you how to have a life and family outside of work while also having a successful career as an engineer. You learned that the gender wage gap and motherhood penalty does exist and how to neutralize it. You learned the critical importance of a home-life support system, the PEACE method for equal sharing of household chores, and the basics of pregnancy and returning to work after a baby. You learned the 5 ways having children increase your productivity at work and enhance your network.

If you put to use the principles taught in this book, your engineering career progression will accelerate more quickly than you can imagine. You will increase your earning potential, and become an influential leader in the companies you work for and in your field. I am so excited for you to continue your journey as a trail-blazing female engineer!

Thank you for joining me on the "She Engineers" journey. I hope you have learned a lot from this book. I hope you have completed the exercises so you can propel yourself to the career of your imagination. If this book has helped and inspired you, please share it with others! If you need help applying what you have learned, taking next steps, or simply want to discuss any of these concepts further, I would love to hear from you! Contact me at stephanie@engineersrising.com.

ACKNOWLEDGEMENTS

There were so many awesome people who helped me write this book and gave me feedback for continuous improvement. Thanks for your support and for helping make this book great!

To my husband Jason—Thank you for your encouragement. Thank you for not thinking I was crazy when I said I wanted to write a book in my non-existent free-time. Thank you for all the evenings shuttling kids around, doing laundry, and generally keeping the household running while I was writing. This book would not have been possible without you.

To my parents—Tim and Lynn—Thank you for all the life lessons you have taught me, which gave me the confidence to do crazy things like become an engineer and write this book. You taught me that anything is possible if I set my mind to it and am willing to work hard.

To the Self-Publishing School (SPS) community—Thank you, Chandler Bolt, for creating a step-by-step process where non-writers (and yes, even engineers!) can learn to write and publish a book. Thank you, Sean Sumner and other SPS staff, for facilitating such a supportive online community. The mastermind community is one of the most engaged, encouraging communities in cyberspace. Everyone is so helpful in providing feedback and assistance. You have saved me from myself (and many newbie book writing mistakes) numerous times. Thank you!

To my launch team—thank you for your support and taking time out of your busy lives to spread the message. Your feedback and stories are invaluable. This book is successful because of you!

ABOUT THE AUTHOR

Stephanie is a structural engineer on a mission to help other female engineers create extraordinary careers. She believes that all women have the power to create their own destiny by knowing themselves and using their individual strengths to achieve career and life success.

Stephanie's engineering background is in the construction industry where she has spent the last 15 years designing structures for buildings in the healthcare, retail, and higher education sectors. She has been involved in the design of buildings that have withstood hurricanes, blizzards, and earthquakes. She graduated with an integrated bachelor's and master's in architectural engineering in 2002 and is a licensed professional engineer in multiple states. She has extensive experience as a project manager, where she has learned critical importance of mastering communication skills.

Stephanie loves being involved in industry outreach, meeting other current or prospective engineers (of all genders), and is the current chair of the American Society of Civil Engineers Structural Engineering Institute's Business Practices committee.

Stephanie is also the mother of three daughters and is a wife to her very supportive (also an engineer) husband, Jason.

POST SCRIPT—
HOW I WROTE THIS BOOK

One year ago, I could never have dreamed that I would be sitting here today with a published book. This book could not have been written without the step-by-step instructions from Chandler Bolt's Self-Publishing School (SPS). The inspiration and support of the SPS community staff and members has been invaluable in the writing and publication of this book. Thank you!

If you have ever thought of writing and publishing your own book, I encourage you to visit the link below for Self-Publishing School.

NOW IT'S YOUR TURN

https://xe172.isrefer.com/go/sps4fta-vts/bookbrosinc2647

URGENT PLEA!

Thank you for reading She Engineers!
I hope you have found the information
in this book helpful in crafting the
engineering career of your dreams.

Your opinion and feedback is very important!
I love to hear what you have to say.

I need your input to make the next
version better and spread the word
to other female engineers.

**Please leave a helpful REVIEW
on Amazon letting me know what you thought of the book.**

Thanks so much!!!

~Stephanie

REFERENCES

[1] Dizikes, Peter. 2014. "Workplace Diversity Can Help the Bottom Line." http://news.mit.edu/2014/workplace-diversity-can-help-bottom-line-1007.

[2] National Science Foundation, National Center for Science and Engineering Statistics. 2017. "Women, Minorities, and Persons with Disabilities in Science and Engineering: 2017." https://www.nsf.gov/statistics/2017/nsf17310/data.cfm.

[3] Adams, Rebecca. 2014. "40 Percent Of Female Engineers Are Leaving The Field. This Might Be Why." *Huffington Post*, August 12. http://www.huffingtonpost.com/2014/08/12/female-engineers_n_5668504.html.

[4] Friedman, Ron. 2015. *"The Best Place to Work: The Art and Science of Creating an Extraordinary Workplace.* TarcherPerigee.

[5] Gallup, Inc. 2017. "State of the American Workplace." Poll report, Gallup. http://news.gallup.com/reports/199961/7.aspx.

[6] Metropolitian Life. 1980. "Optimism = Sales Success: A Metropolitian Life Case Study." Case Study. Source: http://www.mindresources.net/marketing/website/profilingtools/MetLifeCaseStudyMRSSS.pdf.

[7] Anchor, Shawn, and Michelle Gielan. 2005. "Consuming negative news can make you less effective at work." Harvard Business Review. https://hbr.org/2015/09/consuming-negative-news-can-make-you-less-effective-at-work.

[8] B.L. Fredrickson, phD. 2011. "Open Hearts Build Lives: Positive Emotions, Induced Through Loving-Kindness Meditation, Build Consequential Personal Resources." Personal Social Psychology. https://www.ncbi.nlm.nih.gov/pmc/articles/PMC3156028/.

[9] Seligman, Martin, Randal Ernst, Jane Gillham, Karen Reivich, and Mark Linkins. 2009. "Positive education: positive psychology and classroom interventions." Oxford Review of Education 35 (3): 293-311.

[10] Oppezzo, and Schwartz. 2014. "Learning, Memory, and Cognition." Journal of Experimental Psychology.

[11] Kolowich, Lindsay. 2015. "The Productivity Diet: What to Eat to Get More Done in a Day." *Hubspot.com*, June 22. Accessed September 19, 2017. https://blog.hubspot.com/marketing/productivity-diet#sm.0001axuzv4sw6ezjqh31narvw2yjm.

[12] Oaklander, Mandy. 2016. "The New Science of Exercise." Time Magazine (Special Edition), September 12. Accessed September 17, 2017. http://time.com/4475628/the-new-science-of-exercise/.

[13] Grant, Adam. 2014. *Give and Take: Why Helping Others Drives Our Success.* Penguin Books.

[14] Mundy, Liza. 2017. "Why is Silicon Valley So Awful to Women?" April. Accessed August 16, 2017. https://www.theatlantic.com/magazine/archive/2017/04/why-is-silicon-valley-so-awful-to-women/517788/.

[15] Irwin, Neil. 2016. "How to Become a C.E.O.? The quickest path is a winding one." *New York Times*, September 9. https://www.nytimes.com/2016/09/11/upshot/how-to-become-a-ceo-the-quickest-path-is-a-winding-one.html?rref=collection%2Fsectioncollection%2Fupshot&action=click&contentCollection=upshot&region=rank&module=package&version=highlights&contentPlacement=1&pgtyp.

[16] Inam, Henna. 2015. *Wired for Authenticity: Seven Practices to Inspire, Adapt, & Lead.* iUniverse.

[17] Wikipedia. 2017. "Ben Franklin Effect." Accessed September 19, 2017. https://en.wikipedia.org/wiki/Ben_Franklin_effect.

[18] McKinsley and Lean-In.Org. 2016. "Women in the Workplace." Accessed September 9, 2017. http://www.mckinsey.com/business-functions/organization/our-insights/women-in-the-workplace-2016.

[19] NCEES. 2017. "Pass rates." Accessed May 13, 2017. http://ncees.org/engineering/se/.

[20] Sandberg, Sheryl. 2013. *Lean In: Women, Work, and the Will to Lead.* Knopf.

[21] McGinn, Kathleen L, and Nicole Tempest. 2000. "Heidi Roizen." Harvard Business School Case 800-228. http://www.hbs.edu/faculty/Pages/item.aspx?num=26880.

[22] Weir, Kirsten. 2013. "Feel like a fraud?" gradPSYCH (American Psychological Association), November 13. Accessed May 6, 2017. http://www.apa.org/gradpsych/2013/11/fraud.aspx .

[23] Cokley, Kevin, Shannon McClain, Alicia Enciso, and Mercedes Martinez. 2013. "An Examination of the Impact of Minority Status Stress and Impostor Feelings on the Mental Health of Diverse Ethnic Minority College Students." Journal of Multicultural Counseling and Development 4 (2): 82-95. Accessed May 7, 2017. http://onlinelibrary.wiley.com/doi/10.1002/j.2161-1912.2013.00029.x/full.

[24] Goldhill, Olivia. 2016. "Is imposter syndrome a sign of greatness?" Quartz, February 1. Accessed September 17, 2017. https://qz.com/606727/is-imposter-syndrome-a-sign-of-greatness/.

[25] Huston, Cate. 2015. "The Trouble with Imposters." Model view culture, April 28. Accessed May 20, 2017. https://modelviewculture.com/pieces/the-trouble-with-imposters.

[26] Shell, Jasmine. 2017. "Are you an impostor?" Lloyd's Market Association. Accessed June 16, 2017. http://www.lmalloyds.com/LMA/Young_Professionals/Connections/LMA/Young_Professionals/Newsletter/Impostor_Syndrome.aspx.

[27] Wikipedia. 2015. "Deepwater Horizon Oil Spill." Accessed September 2, 2017. https://en.wikipedia.org/wiki/Deepwater_Horizon_oil_spill.

[28] Walsh, Bryan. 2010. "Oil Spill: Goodbye, Mr. Hayward." Time Magazine, July 25. Accessed September 2, 2017. http://science.time.com/2010/07/25/oil-spill-goodbye-mr-hayward/.

[29] Savage , Merle, and Amy Goodman. 2010. "BP Oil Spill Cleanup Workers Getting Sick, Exxon Valdez Survivor Warns of Long-Term Health Effects (Interview)." July 7. Accessed September 2, 2017. https://www.democracynow.org/2010/7/7/bp_oil_spill_cleanup_workers_getting.

[30] Adams, Susan. 2014. "The 10 Skills Employers Most Want In 2015 Graduates." Forbes, November 12. https://www.forbes.com/sites/susanadams/2014/11/12/the-10-skills-employers-most-want-in-2015-graduates/#110a1da32511.

[31] Donnell, Jeffrey A., Betsy M. Aller, Michael Alley, and April A Kedrowicz. 2011. "AC 2011-1503: WHY INDUSTRY SAYS THAT ENGINEERING GRADUATES." American Society for Engineering Education. https://agency.zerys.com/ProjectTitleAttachment/engineering_industry_communication_final122716.pdf.

[32] Perelman, Leslie C, James Paradis, and Edward Barrett. 2001. *The Mayfield Handbook of Technical and Science Writing*. The McGraw-Hill. Source: The Mayfield handbook of technical and science writing. http://www.mhhe.com/mayfieldpub/tsw/eff-char.htm.

[33] Fasano, Anthony. 2015. "TECC63: Engineering Communication Skills: The 7 deadly sins and how to overcome them (Podcast Interview)." Accessed September 4, 2017. https://engineeringcareercoach.com/tag/skip-weisman/.

[34] Cleaver, Jamie. 2012. "Why do engineers struggle to communicate?" Institution of Chemical Engineers. Accessed September 4, 2017. https://www.youtube.com/watch?v=Wm0jNmRST-w.

[35] Buchanan, Leigh. 2016. "The Most Productive Teams at Google Have These 5 Dynamics." *Inc.*, April 12. https://www.inc.com/leigh-buchanan/most-productive-teams-at-google.html.

[36] Deltek in collaboration with ACEC. 2013. Architecture and Engineering Industry Study: 34th annual comprehensive report. Deltek. Accessed September 7, 2017. https://network.aia.org/HigherLogic/System/DownloadDocumentFile.ashx?DocumentFileKey=a5a166a9-f7d8-4476-8615-4bbf20506ec6.

[37] Bradberry, Travis. 2014. "Emotional Intelligence - EQ." Forbes, January 9. Accessed September 6, 2017. https://www.forbes.com/sites/travisbradberry/2014/01/09/emotional-intelligence/#3caed17e1ac0.

[38] Adshead-Grant, Jane. "Listen Like Oprah ." Blog, janeadsheadgrant.com. Accessed September 6, 2017. http://janeadsheadgrant.com/listen-like-oprah/.

[39] Rath, Tom. 2004. "The Impact of Positive Leadership." Gallup News, May 13. Accessed September 16, 2017. http://news.gallup.com/businessjournal/11458/impact-positive-leadership.aspx.

[40] Martinuzzi, Bruna. 2014. "How Successful People Stay Calm Under Pressure." American Express. Accessed September 6, 2017. https://www.americanexpress.com/us/small-business/openforum/articles/6-ways-successful-people-stay-calm-pressure/.

[41] Morgan, Angie, and Lynch, Courtney. 2006. *Lead from the Front: No excuse leadership tactics for women*. McGraw-Hill Education.

[42] Reynolds, Gretchen. 2013. "How Exercise Can Calm Anxiety." New York Times , July 3. Accessed September 16, 2017. https://well.blogs.nytimes.com/2013/07/03/how-exercise-can-calm-anxiety/.

[43] Basu, Tanya. 2014. "Timeline: A History of GM's Ignition Switch Defect." National Public Radio (npr.org), March 31. Accessed September 17, 2017. http://www.npr.org/2014/03/31/297158876/timeline-a-history-of-gms-ignition-switch-defect.

[44] Atiyeh, Clifford. 2015. "GM Ignition-Switch Review Complete: 124 Fatalities, 274 Injuries." Car and Driver, August 3. Accessed September 16, 2017. http://blog.caranddriver.com/GM-IGNITION-SWITCH-REVIEW-COMPLETE-124-FATALITIES-274-INJURIES/.

[45] Gallo, Carmine. 2014. "Two Misleading Words Triggered GM's Catastrophic Communication Breakdown." Forbes, June 9. Accessed September 16, 2017. https://www.forbes.com/sites/carminegallo/2014/06/09/two-misleading-words-triggered-gms-catastrophic-communication-breakdown/#2f840f605ca0.

[46] Hewlett, Sylvia. 2014. *Executive Presence: The Missing Link Between Merit and Success*. HarperCollins Publishers.

[47] Nisen, Max. 2013. "Male CEOs with Deeper Voices Run Bigger Companies and Make More Money." Business Insider Australia, April 19. https://www.businessinsider.com.au/voice-pitch-and-success-2013-4.

[48] Wake Forest University Baptist Medical Center. 2001. "Americans Speak Out, Select the 'Best and Worst Voices in America'." Center for Voice Disorders , Wake Forest University, Winston-Salem, NC. http://www.nrcdxas.org/articles/voices.html.

[49] Lowen, Linda. 2017. "Do Women With Lower Voice Pitch Have More Authority, Achieve Greater Success?" ThoughtCo.com, May 29. Accessed 10 29, 2017. https://www.thoughtco.com/women-lower-voice-pitch-authority-success-3533843.

[50] Schumann, Karina. 2011. "When and Why Women Apologize More than Men." PhD Thesis, Psychology, University of Waterloo, Waterloo, Ontario, Canada. https://uwspace.uwaterloo.ca/bitstream/handle/10012/5998/Schumann_Karina.pdf?sequence=1.

[51] Daly, Annie. 2015. "How Many Times a Day Do You Say "Sorry"?" Women's Health, Feburary 2. Accessed 10 29, 2017. https://www.womenshealthmag.com/life/saying-sorry-too-much.

[52] Seinfeld, Jerry. 1992. Seinfeld TV show (exerpt). Castle Rock Entertainment. Accessed 10 29, 2017. https://www.youtube.com/watch?v=kL7fTLjFzAg.

[53] Goman, Carol Kinsey. 2011. "5 Body Language Secrets Every Leader Should Know." Forbes, April 19. Accessed 10 29, 2017. HTTPS://WWW.FORBES.COM/SITES/CAROLKINSEYGOMAN/2011

/04/19/5-BODY-LANGUAGE-SECRETS-EVERY-LEADER-SHOULD-KNOW/#7FB5D83E21BB.

[54] Cuddy, Amy. 2015. *Presence*. Little, Brown and Company

[55] Burke, Kenneth. 2016. Blog post. "How Many Emails Do People Get Every Day?" October 11. Accessed 10 29, 2017. https://www.textrequest.com/blog/how-many-emails-do-people-get-every-day/.

[56] Beatty, Kimberely. 2010. "The Math Behind the Networking Claim." Accessed October 31, 2017. http://blog.jobfully.com/2010/07/the-math-behind-the-networking-claim/.

[57] Adler, Lou. 2016. "New Survey Reveals 85% of All Jobs are Filled Via Networking." *LinkedIn.com*. Accessed October 31, 2017. https://www.linkedin.com/pulse/new-survey-reveals-85-all-jobs-filled-via-networking-lou-adler/.

[58] Clark, Dorie. 2015. *Stand Out Networking: A Simple and Authentic Way to Meet People on Your Own Terms*. Portfolio.

[59] Mandossian, Alex. 2016. "How To Become A Networking Master." Accessed October 31, 2017. http://www.alexmandossian.com/2012/01/05/how-to-become-a-networking-master/ .

[60] Willis J, Todorov A. 2006. "First impressions: making up your mind after a 100-ms exposure to a face." Psychological Science 592-8. https://www.ncbi.nlm.nih.gov/pubmed/16866745.

[61] Empowered by Color. 2015. "The Power in Clothing and Color Choices." Accessed October 31, 2017. http://www.empower-yourself-with-color-psychology.com/job-interviews.html.

[62] Groth, Aimee. 2012. "You're The Average Of The Five People You Spend The Most Time With." Business Insider. Accessed November 02, 2017. http://www.businessinsider.com/jim-rohn-youre-the-average-of-the-five-people-you-spend-the-most-time-with-2012-7.

[63] Paquette, Danielle. 2016. "Young women are still less likely to negotiate a job offer. But why?" Washington Post. Accessed November 02, 2017. https://www.washingtonpost.com/news/wonk/wp/2016/07/07/young-women-are-still-less-likely-to-negotiate-a-job-offer-but-why/?utm_term=.d7d42d3307c0.

[64] Hannah Riley Bowles, Linda Babcock, Lei Lai. 2006. "Social incentives for gender differences in the propensity to intitiate negotiations: Sometimes it does hurt to ask." Science Direct. Accessed November 2, 2017. https://www.cfa.harvard.edu/cfawis/bowles.pdf.

[65] McKinsey and LeanIn.Org. 2016. "Women in the Workplace 2016." McKinsey and Company. https://community.oracle.com/docs/DOC-1006810.

[66] Lauren Noel, Christie Hunter Arscott. n.d. "ICDER Executive Report: Millennial Women." Accessed November 02, 2017. https://www.icedr.org/research/documents/15_millennial_women.pdf.

[67] Krawcheck, Sallie. 2017. *Own It: The Power of Women at Work*. Crown Business.

[68] Nawalkha, Ajit. 2017. "What Is Your Strong Weakness." Accessed November 02, 2017. https://www.youtube.com/watch?v=lJm5ez-dq2o.

[69] Marshall Goldsmith, Mark Reiter. 2007. *What Got You Here Won't Get You There: How Successful People Become Even More Successful*. Hachette Books.

[70] Zarya, Valentina. 2016. "The Percentage of Female CEOs in the Fortune 500 Drops to 4%." *Fortune*, June 2016. Accessed November 3, 2017. http://fortune.com/2016/06/06/women-ceos-fortune-500-2016/.

[71] Wechsler, Pat. 2015. "58 women CFOs in the Fortune 500: Is this progress?" *Fortune*, February 24. Accessed November 03, 2017. http://fortune.com/2015/02/24/58-women-cfos-in-the-fortune-500-is-this-progress/.

[72] Dishman, Lydia. 2015. "What The Top CEOs Have In Common." *Fast Company*, November 3. Accessed November 3, 2017. https://www.fastcompany.com/3052915/what-the-top-ceos-have-in-common.

[73] Melissa Artabane, Julie Coffman, Darci Darnell. 2017. "Charting the Course: Getting Women to the Top." *Insights*, January 31. Accessed 11 03, 2017. http://www.bain.com/publications/articles/charting-the-course-women-on-the-top.aspx.

[74] Justin M. Berg, Jane E. Dutton, Amy Wrzesniewski. 2007. "What is Job Crafting and Why Does It Matter?" From the Center for Positive Organizational Scholarship, Michigan Ross School of Business. Accessed 11 03, 2017. http://positiveorgs.bus.umich.edu/wp-content/uploads/What-is-Job-Crafting-and-Why-Does-it-Matter1.pdf.

[75] Structural Engineerings Association California. 2016. "SE3 Survey Report." San Francisco. Accessed 11 03, 2017. http://www.se3project.org/uploads/8/9/5/2/89527265/se3_2016_survey_report.pdf.

[76] Herscher, Penny. 2014. "Twice as Many Women Drop out of Tech as Men. How Can We Stop This From Happening?" Medium Corporation. Accessed 11 04, 2017. https://women2.com/stories/2014/06/30/women-leaving-tech.

[77] Catherine Ashcraft, Sarah Blithe. April 2010. "Women in IT: The Facts." National Center for Women & Information Technology (NCWIT). Accessed 11 04, 2017. http://www.ncwit.org/sites/default/files/legacy/pdf/NCWIT_TheFacts_rev2010.pdf.

[78] National Science Foundation "Table 5-1: Bachelor's Degrees awarded, by sex and by field, 2004-2014." Accessed 11 04, 2017. https://www.nsf.gov/statistics/2017/nsf17310/static/data/tab5-1.pdf.

[79] National Center for Science and Engineering Statistics. 2017. "Women, Minorities, and Persons with Disabilities in Science and Engineering: 2017." Special Report NSF 17-310, National Science Foundation. Accessed 11 04, 2017. https://www.nsf.gov/statistics/2017/nsf17310/data.cfm.

[80] United States Department of Labor. 2016. "Labor Force Participate Rate by Sex, Race, and Hispanic ethnicity, 1948-2016 averages." Women's Bureau. Accessed 11 03, 2017. https://www.dol.gov/wb/stats/NEWSTATS/facts/women_lf.htm#two.

[81] Fleur, Nicholas St. 2014. "Many Women Leave Engineering, Blame The Work Culture." National Public Radio (npr.org), August 12. Accessed 11 04, 2017. http://www.npr.org/sections/alltechconsidered/2014/08/12/339638726/many-women-leave-engineering-blame-the-work-culture.

[82] Zarya, Valentina. 2016. "The Reason So Many Women Leave Engineering Has Nothing to Do With Kids." Fortune, August 24. Accessed 11 4, 2017. http://fortune.com/2016/08/24/women-leave-engineering/.

[83] Zazulia, Nicholas. 2016. "Women Leave STEM Jobs for the Reasons Men Want To." US News and World Report, April 8. Accessed 11 04, 2017. https://www.usnews.com/news/articles/2016-04-08/study-women-leave-stem-jobs-for-the-reasons-men-only-want-to.

[84] Beninger, Anna. 2014. "High Potentials in Tech-Intensive Industries: The Gender Divide in Business Roles". Catalyst. Accessed 11 04, 2017. http://www.catalyst.org/system/files/high_potentials_in_tech-intensive_industries_the_gender_divide_in_business_roles_2.pdf.

[85] Corinne A. Moss-Racusina, John F. Dovidiob, Victoria L. Brescollc, Mark J. Grahama, Jo Handelsmana. n.d. "Science faculty's subtle gender biases favor male students." Proceedings of the National Academy of Sciences of The United States of America. Washington, DC. Accessed 11 04, 2017. http://www.pnas.org/content/109/41/16474.abstract.

[86] Catherine Hill, Christianne Corbett. 2015. "Solving the Equation: The Variables for Women's Success in Engineering and Computing." American Association of University Women, Washington DC. Accessed 11 04, 2017. https://www.aauw.org/research/solving-the-equation/.

[87] Jarrett, Christian. 2014. "The Neuroscience of Decision Making Explained in 30 Seconds." Science, 03 10. Accessed 11 04, 2017. https://www.wired.com/2014/03/neuroscience-decision-making-explained-30-seconds/.

[88] Amy J. C. Cuddy, Peter Glick, Anna Beninger. 2011. "The Dynamics of Warmth and Competence Judgments, and their Outcomes in Organizations." Research in Organizational Behavior 73-98. Accessed 11 04, 2017. http://www.people.hbs.edu/acuddy/in%20press,%20cuddy,%20glick,%20&%20beninger,%20ROB.pdf.

[89] Kay, Katty and Shipman, Claire. 2014. "The Confidence Gap." The Atlantic, May. Accessed 11 04, 2017. https://www.theatlantic.com/magazine/archive/2014/05/the-confidence-gap/359815/.

[90] Groth, Aimee. 2011. "Sheryl Sandberg: 'The Most Important Career Choice You'll Make Is Who You Marry'." Business Insider, 12 01. Accessed 11 04, 2017. http://www.businessinsider.com/sheryl-sandberg-career-advice-to-women-2011-12.

[91] Kopf, Dan. 2015. "What Professions Are Most Likely To Marry Each Other?" Priceonomics , September 16. Accessed 11 04, 2017. https://priceonomics.com/what-professions-are-most-likely-to-marry-each/

[92] Robinson, Joe. 2014. "The Secret to Increased Productivity: Taking Time Off." Entrepreneur Magazine, October. Accessed 11 04, 2017. https://www.entrepreneur.com/article/237446.

[93] Garcia, Cardiff. 2015. "The remarkable productivity stagnation of the US construction sector." The Financial Times Limited, April 15. Accessed 11 04, 2017. https://ftalphaville.ft.com/2014/04/15/1821522/the-remarkable-productivity-stagnation-of-the-us-construction-sector/.

[94] PayScale, Inc. 2017. "Gap Analysis: What Equal Pay Day Gets Wrong." Seattle, WA. Accessed 11 04, 2017. https://www.payscale.com/data-packages/gender-pay-gap.

[95] Coe, Alexis. 2013. "Being Married Helps Professors Get Ahead, but Only If They're Male." The Atlantic, 01 17. Accessed 11 04, 2017. https://www.theatlantic.com/sexes/archive/2013/01/being-married-helps-professors-get-ahead-but-only-if-theyre-male/267289/.

[96] Dishman, Lydia. 2015. "What The Gender Pay Gap Looks Like By Industry." Fast Company, 11 05. Accessed 11 04, 2017. https://www.fastcompany.com/3053226/what-the-gender-pay-gap-looks-like-by-industry.

[97] Parker, Kim, and Gretchen Livingston. 2017. "6 facts about American fathers." Facttank News in Numbers, Pew Research Center. Accessed 11 04, 2017. http://www.pewresearch.org/fact-tank/2017/06/15/fathers-day-facts/.

[98] National Partnership for Women & Families. 2017. "Paid Leave." Washington, DC. Accessed 11 04, 2017. http://www.nationalpartnership.org/issues/work-family/paid-leave.html.

[99] United States Department of Labor. 2000. "Impact of Family and Medical Leave on Non-covered Establishments." Wage and Hour Division, Washington, DC. Accessed 11 04, 2017. https://www.dol.gov/whd/fmla/chapter7.htm.

[100] The Organisation for Economic Co-operation and Development (OECD). 2017. "PF2.1 Key characteristics of parental leave systems." OECD Family Database, Paris, France: The Organisation for Economic Co-operation and Development (OECD). Accessed 11 04, 2017. http://www.oecd.org/els/family/database.htm

[101] Budig, Michelle. 2014. "The Fatherhood Bonus and The Motherhood Penalty: Parenthood and the Gender Gap in Pay." Third Way , September 02. Accessed 11 04, 2017. http://www.thirdway.org/report/the-fatherhood-bonus-and-the-motherhood-penalty-parenthood-and-the-gender-gap-in-pay.

91576919R00115

Made in the USA
Columbia, SC
19 March 2018